The road to spiritual-self-discovery - from egotism or addictions-recovery to God-Consciousness is always ...

"AN INSIDE JOB"

Ronald R. Quesnel
&
Eric E. Borrett

Order this book online at www.trafford.com
or email orders@trafford.com

Most Trafford titles are also available at major online book retailers.

Note for Librarians: A cataloguing record for this book is available from Library
and Archives Canada at www.collectionscanada.ca/amicus/index-e.html

Printed in Victoria, BC, Canada.

ISBN: 978-1-4251-9068-2

*Our mission is to efficiently provide the world's finest, most comprehensive book publishing
service, enabling every author to experience success. To find out how to publish your book, your
way, and have it available worldwide, visit us online at www.trafford.com*

Trafford rev. 12/14/09

 www.trafford.com

North America & international
toll-free: 1 888 232 4444 (USA & Canada)
phone: 250 383 6864 ♦ fax: 812 355 4082

Spiritual Quotes & Acknowledgements of Gratitude

"It is written in the prophets, "And they shall all be taught by God." Every man therefore that has heard, and has learned of the Father, comes unto me. – John 6:45

"The Spirit of the Lord God is upon me. He has anointed me to preach the good news to the poor. He has sent me to heal the broken hearted; to preach deliverance to the captives; and recovering of sight to the blind; to set at liberty those that are wounded; and to preach that now is the acceptable year of the Lord. Today as I speak these words, this Scripture is fulfilled in your hearing." – Luke 4:18. 19, 21

"You have not chosen me. I have chosen you, and ordained you, that you should go and bring forth fruit; and that your fruit should remain; that whatsoever you shall ask of the Father in my name, he will give it to you." - John 15:16

"And they shall build the old wastes, they shall raise up the former desolations, and they shall repair the waste cities, the desolations of many generations…. And you shall be named the Priests of the Lord: men shall call you Ministers of our God." Isaiah 61:4, 6

"Bless the Lord, O my soul, and all that is within me, and forget not all his benefits: who forgives all your mistakes; who heals all your diseases; who redeems your life from destruction; who crowns you with loving kindness And tender mercies; who satisfies your desires with good things, so that your youth is renewed like an eagle." - Psalm 103 :1-5

"It is written in your law, I have said you are gods; you are all sons and daughters of the Most High God." (Psalm 82:6; John 10:34)

"You have absolute control over but one thing and that is your thoughts – this is the most significant and inspiring of all facts known to man. It reflects man's divine nature. This divine power is the sole means by which you may control your own destiny." – Napoleon Hill

We acknowledge the guidance of our Father Mother God in developing and sharing this universal 4-Stage spiritual-self discovery-recovery program. We are grateful for the loving contribution of the dear mystic authors and friends God has led us to meet in the New Thought Spirituality movement. We thank Spirit-led authors like Emmet Fox, Bill Wilson, Joseph Murphy, Charles Fillmore, Emilie Cady, Stella Terrill Mann, U.S. Andersen, Ernest Holmes. Donald Curtis, Jack Boland, Wayne Dyer, and many others. We also thank our dear friend Linda Stewart, now Ron's wife by the grace of God, who helped us edit and revise this "hand of God book. We also thank our dear friend Wayne Moore for his spiritual and technical assistance.

PREFACE:
WHAT THIS BOOK CAN DO FOR YOU

This Book Reveals the Secret of Your God-Given Spiritual Mental Identity, Powers & Laws of Mind as a Son or Daughter of God.

"It is written in your law, I have said you are gods; you are all sons and daughters of the Most High God." (Psalm 82:6; John 10:34)

Our intention in writing this 'hand of God' book is fourfold. First, we will share with you the revolutionary 4-stage spiritual self-discovery-recovery program which God has helped us to develop over the years, and which is common to, and works for all people worldwide, no matter what their creed, color, sex, or beliefs may be. This New Thought Spirituality and Science of Mind, or addictions-recovery process, is one that Jesus and other mystics have taught us we must each incorporate into our lives in order to individualize and express the Spirit-Mind-Love-Life of God in us all as sons and daughters of God. It consists of applying the 12 common step choices that help us all to change our mind-consciousness from a false, outer-authority directed ego-consciousness to a new and true inner-Spirit guided God-Consciousness identity. A new identity which is absolutely necessary to help us to develop our 12 inner spiritual character trait faculties, or powers of mind disciples, such as love, faith, thought control, creative imagination, and intuitive sixth sense.

With Jesus Christ as our Master Teacher, we will learn about the powers of our conscious and subconscious mind, and to understand how to use our God-given spiritual mental powers and laws of mind to govern our thoughts and relationships. Jesus' liberating New Thought Spirituality will help us to change and reform our old ideas and beliefs about the nature of God, ourselves, our neighbors, and the meaning and purpose of our lives. We will also be empowered by learning how to use the 12 creative ideas or attitudes on the ladder of accomplishment, and most importantly, we will learn how to live in the circle of scientific prayer to make our God-given dreams come true and fulfill our destiny as sons and daughters of God.

Our second reason for writing is to inspire, enlighten and empower you by sharing our own experience of how God has worked in us to redeem and restore our lives. You will learn that God, the Universal Subconscious Master-Mind Intelligence, or Spirit in all of creation, is the only Creator, and that your creative power of thought is the only mover. You will discover that God creates for you exactly what your mind and heart thinks, feels, imagines, desires and believes to be true. You will learn that we live in a mental universe and that your habitual thoughts, imagery and faith convictions, mold, shape and create your life destiny, as revealed to us in the Bible words, "as you think in your heart (your subconscious mind), so shall you be." (Proverbs 23:7) You will learn how to use specific techniques and exercises to help you to discipline and control your inner thoughts and feelings, and let God, who responds to your thoughts, feelings and faith convictions, create them into your outer physical life experiences. As you make direct conscious contact with God through your mind thoughts on a daily prayer and meditation basis you will awaken to discover the great spiritual truth of the ages, that your whole outer physical world conditions and circumstances is the result of your own inner thoughts, imagery, and faith beliefs. You will come to realize and faithfully believe that God, the Universal Master Mind-Love-Life-Spirit in us all, has given us dominion to choose our own lives by giving us His power of free will and creative formative thought.

Our third reason for writing this book is to contribute to all 12-Step spiritual mental growth groups, like Alcoholics Anonymous worldwide, by sharing the insights and wisdom contained within this spiritual self-discovery-recovery program. It is our purpose to help individuals who are sick and tired of living a powerless, egoistic and codependent lifestyle of addictive negative thinking of fear, separation, limitation, lack, sickness, poverty, and despair; and who desire and are willing to change their old beliefs and lives for the better by trusting in a Power greater than themselves. For this reason, we have established our Master-Mind Choices for Freedom support groups worldwide. We also intend to attract many individuals and couples worldwide who have experienced God's miracle-working Power in their lives; who have long term experience working a 12-Step program; and feel called by God to teach this New Thought Spirituality and Science of Mind, or addictions-recovery program. We invite you to come to Victoria, BC to take our one year Counselor-Training Certificate Program and, after graduation, to help us expand God's Spiritual Freedom Centre. Together, we will establish branch offices worldwide in order to help other people recover from the limitations and powerlessness of egotism and codependency, and we will come together as one people in God, to experience the glorious liberty and joyous activity of being sons and daughters of God.

Fourthly, we will discover that Jesus Christ's mission and teachings have been sadly misinterpreted and misrepresented for centuries by religious zealots and man-made false theologies. We will come to know that Jesus never came to set up a 'religion' but to wake us all up to our universal God-given spiritual mental powers and laws of mind, and true identity as sons and daughters of God. Then, we will understand Jesus' New Thought Spirituality and Science of Mind in a new light and a new way. As we do this, we will literally, as Paul said, "no longer be conformed to this world, but be transformed from within by changing our thoughts and renewing our mind." (Romans 12:2). We will be set free from the bondage of egotism and worldly mass mind consciousness, and the slavery of giving our power of choice and belief to any religious, or other outer-authority figures. We will come to know a new spiritual, psychological, and symbolic interpretation of the Bible and other sacred writings, whose characters and stories all symbolize our very selves in our journey of spiritual growth and addictions recovery. By doing so, we will experience the freedom of being inner-Spirit directed by making direct conscious contact with God's Spirit-Mind-Love-Life within us all, without having to go through any fear, guilt, and shame-based religious brokers, who falsely claim to know God and His Word better than you do.

With every step you take in moving from a false outer authority directed ego-self centered consciousness to your true inner Spirit-led God-Consciousness, you will be rocketed into a fourth dimension, a new spiritual state of consciousness, and come to know the unlimited power that is yours. You will realize that your thoughts are things and have the creative and imaginative powers to move God, the Universal Subconscious Mind within you and all creation, who creates for you exactly what you think, imagine, and believe to be true in your heart and mind kingdom. You will be more willing to learn how to work in unity with God's will and purpose for your life. As you let go of your false ego-self worldly identity and codependency and negative thought habits of fear, guilt, and shame-based beliefs, you will experience the freedom of your true spiritual-mental powers and God-Conscious identity. By trusting God as the only Universal Master Mind Love-Life Presence and Power within each and all of us, we will break out of the box of bondage to an egoistic and worldly 'mass mind consciousness,' and our codependent slavery to outer authorities. We will know a new spiritual freedom and a new happiness in God-Consciousness, as Jesus and other mystic sages through the ages have taught us, by giving us the vision to see, the faith to believe, and the courage to do.

Here is the diagram of the 4-stage spiritual self-discovery-recovery program that we will be following throughout the book. God bless you and enjoy this greatest of all adventures - our spiritual self-discovery-recovery journey of soul development as a son or daughter of God!

Ron Quesnel and Eric Borrett

Spiritual Freedom Centre for New Thought Spirituality & Addictions Recovery

A 4-Stage Program of Spiritual Self-Discovery-Recovery & Transformation for Men and Women Worldwide

A 4-STAGE PROGRAM TO LEARN JESUS CHRIST'S NEW THOUGHT SPIRITUALITY & GOD'S UNIVERSAL SPIRITUAL-MENTAL LAWS & POWERS. We will learn how to use our God-given 12 Step Choices & 12 Powers of Mind or Spirit, as well as, our 12 Steps of the circle of prayer & ladder of accomplishment. Our mission is to lead lost souls to God within them to recover their God-given spiritual mental identity-powers & manifest their dreams to love & serve humanity.

4-STAGE STEPS FOR SPIRITUAL SELF-DISCOVERY-RECOVERY CHOICES OR CHANGES OF CONSCIOUSNESS FOR A NEW LIFE

Stage 1 Steps 1-2-3: Our Ego-Deflation & Spiritual Rebirth Experience
We Choose 3 New Foundation Steps to Discover Our Spiritual Identity

1) We choose to admit our powerlessness as egotists; that separated from God our Creator, our life had become unmanageable.
- We choose to surrender our fixed egotistic world beliefs and ideas.
- We choose to let go of our ego-pride, our self-will & self-sufficiency.

2) We choose to believe that a Power greater than ourselves – God, the Universal Master Mind Love Spirit can restore us to sanity.
- We choose to receive God's Loving Presence in our heart and mind.
- We choose to believe God will answer us now, if we ask for His help.

3) We choose to turn our will and our lives over to the care of God, the Universal Master Mind Love Spirit to guide us.
- We choose to put our mind in tune with God's Master Mind ideas.
- We choose to let God mold and shape us in His image and likeness.
- We choose to let God teach us His spiritual laws and mind powers.

Stage 2 Steps 4-5-6: By Changing Our Thoughts, We Change Our Lives
We Choose Only Positive Thoughts to Enter our Mind and Not Negatives

4) We choose to make a searching and fearless moral inventory of ourselves, examine our conscience for Truth and errors ideas/ acts.
- We choose to let go of our fears, resentments, anger, control issues.
- We choose to write down our fears, guilt, shame, and abuse issues.

5) We choose to confess and admit to God, to ourselves, and another human being, the exact nature of our wrongs.
- We choose to ask God to face our secrets with a trusted person.
- We choose to accept God's love and forgiveness in order to be free.

6) We choose to be entirely ready to have God remove all our defects of character and replace them with healthy character traits.
- We choose to let God do for us what we cannot do for ourselves.
- We choose to accept God's forgiveness of our past mistakes, and to ask God to help us change our heart and mind beliefs for good.

4-STAGE CHOICES TO USE OUR GOD-GIVEN LAWS OF MIND & POWERS TO SHAPE OUR SPIRITUAL CHARACTER & FULFILL OUR LIFE PURPOSE

Stage 1 Choices: The Humbling of Our Ego & Faith in God's Spirit-Mind-Love
We Unite Our Mind with God's Universal Mind & Become Inner-Spirit-Directed

1 Law of Humility & Truth sets us free: of my ego without God I can do nothing.
2 Law of Faith: We choose to trust a Loving God Power greater than ourselves.
3 Law of Being: we are spiritual beings with God-Mind powers to create our life.
4 Law of Spiritual Identity: "You are gods, sons & daughters of the Most High."
5 Law of Conscious-Subconscious Mind: As you think in your heart, so are you.
6 Law of Supply & Demand: whatever we desire from God believing, we receive.
7 Law of Forgiveness: We accept God's love and forgive ourselves and all others.
8 Law of Spirit Rebirth: By prayer God is born in our heart and consciousness.
9 Law of Love: All people are sons-daughters of God called to love one another.
10 Law of Grace: Our Father God saves us from our egoistic-world self bondage.
11 Law of Prayer: we make direct conscious contact with God-Mind ideas in us.
12 Law of Thought: the thoughts we think & believe in our heart, we experience.
13 Law of Life-Unity- God is the Only Power individualized in each and all of us.

Stage 2 Choices: The Desert Experience: We Choose to Affirm Good & Deny Evil
The Thoughts We Sow In Our Mind-Heart Kingdom Will Reap Good or Bad Fruit

1 Law of Individuality: God's Spirit-Mind-Love-Life is individualized in us all.
2 Law of Creative Thought: inner thoughts-beliefs cause our outer experiences.
3 Law of Cause & Effect: We live in a mental universe: 'As within, so without.'
4 Law of Affirmation & Denial: we affirm Truth thoughts & deny false beliefs.
5 Law of Becoming Inner-Spirit guided & letting go of being outer authority led.
6 Law of the Lock & Seven Day Mental Diet to change our subconscious beliefs.
7 Law of Freedom of Co-dependency: we can only control our mind, not others.
8 Law of the Mind: We have powers to think, believe, pray, imagine, love, choose.
9 Law of Meditation-Receptivity- we ask, listen & follow our inner God guidance.
10 Law of Forgiveness: God frees us from ego fears, limitation, sickness, poverty.
11 Law of Creative Imagination: we pray, visualize-actualize God ideas into form.
12 Law of Substitution: We choose to replace false beliefs with good God Truths.
13 Law of Attraction: Inner thoughts we believe with faith become outer realities.
14 Law of Will: We will to do God's will - Source of all good ideas-dreams-desires.

Spiritual Freedom Centre - www.spiritualfreedomcentre.com
Copyright Ron Quesnel Counseling Associates 2009

Spiritual Freedom Centre for New Thought Spirituality & Addictions Recovery
A 4-Stage Program of Spiritual Self-Discovery-Recovery & Transformation for Men and Women Worldwide

A 4-STAGE PROGRAM TO LEARN JESUS CHRIST'S NEW THOUGHT SPIRITUALITY & GOD'S UNIVERSAL SPIRITUAL-MENTAL LAWS & POWERS
We will learn how to use our God-given 12 Step Choices & 12 Powers of Mind or Spirit &, our 12 Steps of the circle of prayer & the ladder of accomplishment.
Our mission is to lead lost souls to God within them to recover their God-given spiritual mental identity-powers & manifest their dreams to love & serve humanity.

4-STAGE STEPS FOR SPIRITUAL SELF-DISCOVERY-RECOVERY CHOICES OR CHANGES OF CONSCIOUSNESS FOR A NEW LIFE

4-STAGE CHOICES TO USE OUR GOD-GIVEN LAWS OF MIND & POWERS TO SHAPE OUR SPIRITUAL CHARACTER & FULFILL OUR LIFE PURPOSE

Stage 3 Steps 7-8-9: We Seek Peace with God, Ourselves and Neighbors
Practicing Spiritual traits of love, forgiveness, truth, patience, tolerance

7) We humbly choose to ask God to remove all our shortcomings.
• We choose to let God guide and direct our thoughts, words, deeds.
• We choose to pray daily for love, peace, patience and tolerance.
8) We choose to make a list of all persons we have harmed and become willing to make amends to all of them.
• We choose to accept God's forgiveness and forgive all who hurt us.
• We choose to deal with, and clean up the wreckage of our past.
9) We choose to make direct amends to people wherever possible, except when to do so, would injure them or others.
• We choose to admit our errors and ask others to forgive us.
• We choose to thank God for healing our relationships with peace.

Stage 3 Choices: The Creative Resurrection Experience: Claiming Our God-Powers
We Learn to Use the 12 Steps of Circle of Prayer & Make Our Dreams Come True

1. Law of Spiritual-Mental Healing: put on Mind of Christ and speak the word.
2. Law of Spiritual Individual Identity: you are a unique son or daughter of God.
3. Law of Living in Circle of Prayer to fulfill God's will & dream purpose for us.
4. Law of Forgiveness: we forgive others as God has forgiven us and set us free.
5. Law of Resist not Evil: our mind kingdom accepts only good & denies evil entry
6. Law of Unconditional Love: We think-feel only Good God thoughts towards all.
7. Law of Giving-Receiving: what we sow in inner thought, we reap in outer life.
8. Law of Creative Imagination: we mentally picture our desire as already done.
9. Law of Creative Thought: what we think in our heart, we actualize in our life.
10. Law of Speaking God's Word in us with authority – knowing it will bear fruit.
11. Law of Universal Subconscious Mind-Spirit that forms our ideas into reality.

Stage 4 Steps 10-11-12: Becoming Aware of God's Will-Purpose for Us
We Daily Apply the Spiritual Mental Laws of Mind, Love & Life

10) We choose to take personal inventory, and when we were wrong promptly admitted it, to maintain our peace of mind and serenity.
• We choose to stay aware of our God-given daily guidance.
• We choose to be at peace with our thoughts and all relationships.
11) We choose to seek through prayer & meditation to improve our conscious contact with God as we understand Him, praying only for knowledge of His will for us, and the power to carry that out.
• We choose to pray daily to do God's will – to love and serve all.
• We choose every morning and evening to thank God for His help.
12) Having had a spiritual awakening as a result of these steps, we choose to carry this message to others, and to practice these spiritual-mental principles or laws, in all our affairs.
• We choose to freely receive God's love and pass it on to others.
• Healed by God's Love, we choose to become the wounded healers.

Stage 4 Choices: The Inner Transformative Love-Vision-Mission Experience
We Pass On God's Blessings As the Light of the World, Salt of the Earth

1. Law of God given Talents of love, faith, thinking, imagination, prayer, praise.
2. Law of Speaking our Word of Power to free and heal the wounded and lost.
3. Law of Faith or Belief to manifest our God-given dreams of love & service.
4. Law of Sharing our Stories of God's blessings to give others love, faith & hope.
5. Law of prayer- meditation in God's Presence power to rise above all problems.
6. Law of living a God-centered, inner-Spirit-guided life & teach love by example.
7. Law of claiming our spiritual identity – that God in us all things are possible!
8. Law of Mind – as you think in your heart – subconscious mind- so are you.
9. Law of Identification as sons and daughters of God-Consciousness and powers.
10. Law of accepting God as Source of ideas, dreams, peace, joy, supply, freedom.
11. Law of transforming our scars into healing balm to heal our wounded friends.
12. Law of Redemption: through God's grace we become wounded healers for all.
13. Law of Attraction: We pray daily giving thanks & ask for creative thoughts to love and serve all in the freedom and fellowship of God's Spirit & will for us.
14. Law of becoming a light of the world the salt of the earth & glorify God's Name

Spiritual Freedom Centre c/o Ron Quesnel Counseling Associates Victoria, BC www.spiritualfreedocentre.com

CONTENTS

STAGE I CHOICES

THE HUMBLING OF
OUR FALSE EGO-
SELF-IDENTITY
EXPERIENCE
AND OUR SPIRITUAL
REBIRTH INTO
GOD-CONSCIOUSNESS

4-STAGE STEPS FOR SPIRITUAL SELF DISCOVERY-RECOVERY CHOICES OR CHANGES OF CONSCIOUSNESS FOR A NEW LIFE

<u>**Stage 1 Steps 1-2-3: Our Ego Deflation & Spiritual Rebirth Experience We Choose 3 New Foundation Steps to Discover Our Spiritual-Identity**</u>

1)   We choose to admit our powerlessness as egotists: that separated from God our Creator, our life had become unmanageable.

-   We choose to surrender our fixed egotistic world beliefs and ideas.

-   We choose to let go of our ego-pride, self-will and self-sufficiency.

2)   We choose to believe that a Power greater than ourselves - God, the Universal Master Mind Love Spirit, can restore us to sanity.

-   We choose to receive God's Loving Presence in our heart & mind.

-   We choose to believe God will answer us if we ask for His help.

3)   We choose to turn our will and lives over to the care of God, our Father Mind Mother Love Spirit of the universe to guide us.

-   We choose to put our mind in tune with God's Master Mind ideas.

-   We choose to let God mold and shape us in His image and likeness.

-   We choose to let God teach us His spiritual laws & mind powers.

SPIRITUAL FREEDOM CENTRE – A 4-Stage Program for New Thought Spirituality & Addictions-Recovery

4-STAGE STEPS FOR SPIRITUAL SELF DISCOVERY-RECOVERY CHOICES OR CHANGES OF CONSCIOUSNESS FOR A NEW LIFE

<u>**Stage 1 Choices: Our Ego Humbling & Faith in God's Spirit-Mind-Love We Let God's Love into our Heart and Become Inner-Spirit-Directed**</u>

1 Law of Humility and Truth sets us free: I admit that of my little ego-self, without God, the Master Mind-Spirit, I can do nothing.

2 Law of Faith: We choose to trust a Loving God Power greater than ourselves.

3 Law of Being: We are spiritual beings with God-Mind powers to create our life.

4 Law of Spiritual Identity: "You are gods, sons and daughters of the Most High."

5 Law of Conscious and Subconscious Mind: As you think in your heart, so are you.

6 Law of Supply and Demand: Whatever we desire from God believing, we receive.

7 Law of Forgiveness: We accept God's love and forgive ourselves and all others.

8 Law of Spirit Rebirth: By prayer God is born in our heart and consciousness.

9 Law of Love: All people are sons and daughters of God called to love one another.

10 Law of Grace: Our Father-God saves us from our egoistic-world self bondage.

11 Law of Prayer: We make direct conscious contact with God-Mind ideas in us.

12 Law of Thought: The thoughts we think and believe in our heart, we experience.

13 Law of Life-Unity- God is the Only Power whose Spirit-Mind-Love-Life individualizes in each and all of us.

CHAPTER ONE

STEP CHOICE 1 FOR SPIRITUAL SELF DISCOVERY-RECOVERY

We humbly chose to admit the Truth, that of our false ego-self, separated from God, the Universal Subconscious Master-Mind-Love-Spirit, we were powerless, and that our lives had become unmanageable – that of ourselves without God, our Source, we could do nothing.

THE LOCK: WE ARE ALL PRISONERS IN OUR OWN MIND: OF OUR FALSE AND POWERLESS EGO-MIND-SELF IDENTITY

Without knowing it, without being truly aware or conscious of it, we were living our lives in our small and false ego-self conscious identity and making our choices based on our faith in the beliefs and values of outer authority figures. We had become ego-self-centered, outer-authority-directed individuals. All this seemed to be okay for quite awhile as we grew up. We do, after all, want to fit in, we want to belong, we all want to be accepted. We really do want to please everyone, not hurt anyone, and still we want the freedom to be, and do our own thing, without rocking the boat. Soon, we got caught up in the 'rat race mentality, or ego-consciousness, or outer-oriented world.' Then, as time goes by, we started to notice, slowly or quickly, that as we expressed our own thoughts, ideas, and feelings, our own individuality, there were dire consequences to not obeying, or not conforming to the laws of these outer world authority figures in society, religion, and politics.

This was not so apparent at first, but now we begin to see this more clearly, because our own inner Spirit, that small, still voice of God within us, that has always been there, wants to be listened to, wants to be heard, and obeyed, so we can be at peace, and at one with our true God-given spiritual identity.   Suddenly one day, we wake up, and say something like this: 'O my God,' notice that God is always mentioned, "I have been living my whole life in the box of what my small finite ego-centered-self believes, and the world of outer authorities have told me to believe, to say, to do, and to feel. I have sold my soul, or integrity, because I have conformed all my thoughts, beliefs, dreams, and my very life to outer authority figures, and I didn't know it."

Now we ask ourselves: "What do I believe in? What do I think? What do I want to do with my life? By the way, who am I anyway? Who is God? What is the purpose and meaning of my life?" This is a wake up call! For most of us this has usually been a forty-year journey. 'Forty years in the desert,' in the Bible symbolizes, or means, a long time slavery to the false, negative beliefs we learned from other outer authorities that we unconsciously allowed to run our lives. They passed onto us the learned beliefs and values, behaviors and roles they inherited from their ancestors, the world they grew up in thinking all was true. This experience is true for all of us.

THE KEY: WE HUMBLY ADMIT OUR EGO POWERLESSNESS

Now if you are sick and tired of following the beliefs and behaviors of other outer authorities, of being ego-centered, and have reached the point in your life where you are willing to be honest with yourself from within your own inner-Spirit, then you have already started praying for help. You are ready to look for the Truth within you, inside your own heart and mind, instead of outside yourself. You are now ready and ripe to experience the powers of prayer, humility, and truth. You now admit that of your own ego-self wits, disconnected from God, you have become lost, afraid, scattered, broken, and fearfully alone. You are honestly admitting that you are responsible for your past mistakes, and need the love, and help of a Power greater than yourself to save you from the hell you find yourself in. Hell, by the way, is a state of mind which thinks, "I don't need anybody. Nobody's going to tell me what to do. I know it all. I can do it on my own." Hell is thinking your ego-self is self-sufficient unto itself, and that you don't need the love and help of other people. It is a loveless existence that thinks the world, indeed the very universe, is composed of 'me, myself, and I' alone. It is an ego-centered lie that separates and destroys you.

This idea of separateness from God and other people is the fundamental sin that leads to hell, to aloneness, and isolation from God, other people, and all creation. You want to be an individual, who is free to make your own life choices, and follow your own inner-Spirit guidance and dreams. You want to be to be accepted just as you are, and you want guidance, but where do you find it? This is the question.

We are all Truth-seekers, because Wisdom is in us. We just have not paid attention to it enough. Jesus came to wake us up to this Truth of God's Spirit dwelling in all of us. He said, 'If you listen to my words, you will know the Truth, and the Truth will set you free.' Sooner or later, we each ask ourselves the basic, fundamental questions of life: Who am I? Who and what do I believe? Why was I born? Why am I here? What do I want to do with my life? What can I do to be happy, joyous, prosperous, and free? Where can I go to find the answers my heart is seeking? Who is God? What does God want me to do? How do I listen to the beat of my own drummer, and follow my own heart's desires? How can I be the captain of my own soul and life ship? How can I be at peace with myself, and everybody else? How can I get rid of my low self-esteem, and negative feelings of inferiority and inadequacy? How can I be truly fulfilled and prosperous? If anyone knows, please show me the way, because I am sick and tired, of being sick and tired, and living the way I am.   Can anyone save me from my fears, my feelings of anxiety, uselessness, despair, powerlessness, and from the hell on earth I am experiencing? I am willing to go to any length to find out the answers.   'To be or not to be,' that is the question,' asked Shakespeare.   It is the question we must each and all ask and answer for ourselves!

SHARING A PERSONAL - UNIVERSAL PRODIGAL SON STORY

Like the Prodigal Son in the Bible, who wasted his inheritance 'in riotous living,' you too are worn out.   You have either, 'bottomed out,' 'burned out,' had a 'mental breakdown,' or hit a 'mid-life crisis'.   Whatever you call it, it means you are ready to come home to your true Source.   But, on the other hand, your old ego-self does not want to let go that easily.   It's been in charge of your life for twenty, thirty, forty, or more years.   So it starts with the stinking thinking again: 'Maybe I don't want anybody telling me what to do.   Maybe I can still do this on my own.   Maybe there is no hope for me.   Maybe even God Himself could never forgive me.   Maybe there is no God.   Maybe this idea is ridiculous, and I am just fooling myself. Maybe this freedom is too frightening.   Maybe I'll just be content the way things are.' Then again, you say, 'No! I've already tried all this, and it just doesn't work.   I give up!'

Like the Prodigal Son, you must take a leap of faith, and willingly freely choose to admit the Truth, that you cannot do it on your own, and finally surrender, or let go of your ego-self-centered driven life alone, cut off from God, neighbor, and all creation.   At last, you begin to listen and hear the voice of God's Spirit within you, and then, like the Prodigal Son, 'you come to yourself, (to your senses)' and say … 'I will arise and go to my Father.' You humbly pray, 'Dear God, if you really do exist, please help me! I need your help.   I am willing to go to any lengths to recover my life.   I am lost, scattered, and so afraid and alone.   I accept the Truth that of myself I can do nothing.   Dear God, I am willing to admit, that I am powerless over my life.' Finally, I am willing to let go of my 'greatest possession,' my false belief in self-sufficiency, and ego-self knowledge, and in my 'self-will run riot life.'

We each know, deep down within ourselves, that we have our own individual unique talents and dreams to contribute to make this world a better place. This is God's Spirit-Mind-Love stirring within us that we have ignored in the past, and that now quietly asks for your attention.   It is 'that still small voice of God's Spirit within you,' asking you to listen and hear the good news, that God loves you just as you are, and has placed a dream in your heart even before you were born.   As we grow and learn through trial, error, and suffering, we eventually learn to admit that on our own ego-wits, we are powerless without God, and so we humbly invite Him into our heart, mind and life.   We admit that by our own ego-centered and outer-authority-directed worldly ways, lost in the 'rat race mentality of the world,' we became afraid, lost, scattered, blind, and broken vessels. Now, you are ready to hear what Nicodemus heard from Jesus when he asked, 'What must I do?' And Jesus said, 'You must be born again.' The only solution to our problems is and ever will be a spiritual or God-centered solution.

THE ROAD TO SPIRITUAL SELF-DISCOVERY-RECOVERY

This journey of soul development and discovering your True Spiritual Self Identity as a son or daughter of God will be an "inside job," that will change your life from within for good and forever. It will inspire, enlighten and empower you to live an abundant and fulfilling God-Mind centered, and inner Spirit guided life. However, there is a price to be paid. It requires that we change our old ego and codependent negative thoughts and beliefs, and let go of our destructive fear, guilt and shame-based subconscious feelings, or prompters, that have limited us so much in the past; and replace them with a new self image of positive and affirmative good God-Truth thoughts. This will include reforming our beliefs about God, ourselves, our neighbor and all our relationships. As we turn to God, a Power greater than ourselves, He will help us change from within, to change our inner thinking, heart, and beliefs; then our whole outer life conditions will be renewed, transformed and revitalized. As we progress in this inner work, that only we each can do, we will no longer be the same person, and we will be transformed by the renewing of our mind. As we surrender our false ego identity, and false beliefs, and freely choose to trust in God, we each will see with new eyes, hear with new ears, and think and feel with a new mind and heart. We will be rocketed into a 4th dimensional state of God-Consciousness, and be One in God's Spirit-Mind-Love-Life, and will know a new heaven and a new earth.

All you need to start this journey is the desire and willingness to be honest, open-hearted and open-minded, and do the work suggested. This life renewing adventure will set your Creative Spirit-Mind free in ways you never even dreamed possible. As you continue daily on this journey with God, you'll put on a new identity and become inner Spirit-guided, and discover that God, the Universal Subconscious Master-Mind dwells in your heart and mind and is responsive to your conscious thoughts, beliefs, suggestions, desires and dreams. As you learn to synchronize your conscious and subconscious mind you will discover your God-given powers of mind and life; and you will find your true place and life purpose, and you will know a new freedom and a new happiness that you never dreamed possible. You will be inspired, enlightened, and empowered by God to fulfill your destiny by doing His will or business, which is to be happy, joyous, prosperous and free. You will never be alone again, and you will realize that God needs you and wants to individualize in you to fulfill your heart's desires to love and serve all humanity and contribute and make a difference as a son or daughter of God. This is how you and I glorify God.

HOW OUR NEW THOUGHT SPIRITUALITY PROGRAM WORKS

There are 4-Universal and common stages and step choices, or spiritual mental laws and character trait faculties or powers, that apply to all people worldwide, no matter what our creed, sex, color, or cultural beliefs may be. We will take them one at a time in each chapter in order to discover-recover our true spiritual mental identity, powers, and freedom as sons and daughters of God. Here are the twelve God-given step-choices and 12 spiritual mental faculties, or character trait powers and laws of mind we will explore, take, and incorporate into our lives one at a time as part of our spiritual mental growth, or soul development journey, into God-Consciousness.

Just like 12 Step spiritual growth programs developed by Alcoholics Anonymous groups worldwide this God-given universal spiritual growth program states that: Never have we seen a person fail who has thoroughly followed this spiritual mental growth program. Those who do not recover their true spiritual self identity as sons or daughters of God, are those who do not desire to change and let go of their false ego-self identity, and are not honest with themselves. There are such unfortunates. They are incapable of letting go of their ego, or 'bloated nothingness,' as Emerson so well put it. They are not at fault, but they suffer from the isolation and separation from God, neighbor, and all creation by living in hell, a world of 'me, myself and I alone,' an ego-world conscious mindset without love, and so, without God.

Our stories disclose in a general way what we were like as egotists, what happened, and what we are like now. If you have decided you want what we have and are willing to go to any length to recover your true God-Self identity and spiritual mental powers, and learn how to use the spiritual mental laws of mind, love and life, then you are ready to follow this simple spiritual program. Here are the 12 Step Choices and 12 spiritual-mental character traits powers of mind, love and life suggested as a spiritual program of self-discovery-recovery. At some of these we balked, we thought we could find an easier, softer way, but we could not. So with all the love in our heart and earnestness at our command, we ask you to be fearless and thorough from the very start. Some of us have tried to hold on to our old ideas and beliefs, but the result was nil until we let go absolutely.

Remember that we deal with egotism - cunning, baffling and powerful! Without help it is too much for us. But there is one who has all Power, that One is God, the Universal Subconscious Master-Mind-Love-Spirit, which indwells you and all creation. May you find Him now! Half measures availed us nothing. We asked God's protection and care with complete abandon. We choose to let go completely of our old, false, egoistic, outer authority directed negative beliefs, and take a leap of faith. Our old ego ways of thinking availed us nothing but misery, isolation and despair. We stand at the turning point of our lives. Either we go on trying to do things alone, all by ourself, in our ego-self-existence, or we turn to a Power greater than ourselves, a loving God who has all Power to restore us to sanity, or to our true self identity and spiritual mental powers as sons and daughters of God.

Here on the next pages are the 12 step-choices and 12 powers of mind we suggest you take and develop as a program of spiritual self-discovery-recovery that will change your life for good:

12 MASTER-MIND STEP-CHOICES FOR SPIRITUAL FREEDOM

12 Common Universal Step-Choices to Change Our Consciousness and Build Our Spiritual Character Traits or Powers of Mind

1. We humbly chose to admit the Truth, that of our false ego-self separated from God, the Universal Subconscious Master-Mind-Love-Spirit, we were powerless, and that our lives had become unmanageable – that of ourselves, without God, our Source and Creator, we could do nothing.

2. We freely chose to believe or have faith that a loving God, a Power greater than ourselves, in whose Creative Universal Subconscious Master-Mind-Love-Spirit we all live and move and have our being, could restore us to sanity by uniting us in the fellowship of His Spirit-Mind-Love-Life.

3. We chose or made the decision to turn our will and our lives over to the care of God, the Universal Subconscious Master-Mind-Love-Spirit dwelling in the heart-mind kingdom of us all, to guide us in His will to our life purpose which is nothing less than our heart's desire to love, contribute, and serve humanity.

4. We chose to make a searching and fearless moral inventory of ourselves by using a seven day mental diet. We learned how to affirm only good God-thoughts to enter our mind-heart kingdom, and to deny entry to negative false thoughts and beliefs. We learned to be set free from the prison of our past negative ego-self thinking. We were transformed by the renewing of our mind, and our God-given creative power of thought control.

5. We chose to admit to God, to ourselves, and to another human being the exact truth of our past negative thinking ego-fears and attitudes. To let them go by becoming inner-Spirit-directed, and recovering our true spiritual self-identity by letting God renew and restore our mind, thoughts, beliefs, and our entire life.

6. We chose to be entirely ready and willing to have God remove all our negative character defects, to change our thinking from ego to God-Consciousness, and to inspire, enlighten, and empower us to use our spiritual mental faculties and laws of mind to fulfill His will and God-given dreams for us and all humanity.

7. We humbly chose to ask our Father-Mind Mother-Love God within us, to remove our shortcomings by praying daily in His Presence, and living in the circle of prayer or God-Consciousness, to fulfill His will or dream purpose for us, so we can have a happy, joyous and free creative love life.

8. We chose to accept God's love and forgiveness for our mistakes, and became willing to make amends to all whom we had harmed and had harmed us so we could be at peace with all people, and focus on fulfilling God's will and love-dream purpose for us and the good of all humanity.

9. We chose to trust God's Inner-Spirit guidance and were given the courage to make amends to all people we had harmed to heal all our relationships and be at peace with all. As we did so we let go of our ego- separation from others and entered into the unity and fellowship of God's One Universal Subconscious Master-Mind-Love-Spirit as sons or daughters.

10. We chose to take a daily personal inventory of ourselves by seeking God's inner-Spirit guidance, and power to control our heart and mind kingdom. We sow only good God-thought seeds and deny entry promptly to any negative mental poison-thoughts into the garden of our heart-mind, in order to maintain our new spiritual identity, unity, and fellowship as sons and daughters of God.

11. We chose by daily prayer and meditation to make direct conscious contact with God's Infinite Mind and Boundless Love within our subconscious mind, praying only for the knowledge of our Father-Mother God's will, or love dream purpose to fulfill our lives, and the Power to carry that out by claiming our God-given spiritual mental powers and identity as sons and daughters of God.

12. Having had a spiritual awakening by God setting us free from our false ego-self identity to God-Consciousness as a result of these faith step-choices, we recovered our true spiritual mental identity, faculties, and laws of mind as sons and daughters of God, and chose to share this good news to free other egotists separated from God, and to practice these laws or principles in all our affairs.

12 SPIRITUAL MENTAL CHARACTER TRAITS, OR POWER OF MIND FACULTIES TAUGHT BY JESUS & SYMBOLIZED AS OUR 12 DISCIPLES

Note: * This Spirit-led discovery was found by Ron Quesnel, as an answer to prayer, in Emmet Fox's book "The Sermon on the Mount," Joseph Murphy's book "The Power of Your Subconscious Mind," the Big Book of "Alcoholics Anonymous, Charles Fillmore's book "The Twelve Powers of Man," and Jack Boland's tapes on "The Transforming System," and of course in the Bible, and many other New Thought Spirituality or Science of Mind authors - both past and contemporary. This entire program has been developed as an answer to prayer to set God's people free from the bondage to false ego-centered worldly beliefs or outer authorities by trusting God within us and becoming 'inner-Spirit directed' sons and daughters of God.

DIAGRAM OF 12 SPIRITUAL MENTAL POWERS OF
MAN – CHARACTER TRAITS

Here are the six common masculine (intellectual) and six feminine (feeling) God-given spiritual mental character trait faculties we all need to develop in order to break out of the box of our false ego-self and become sons and daughters of God.

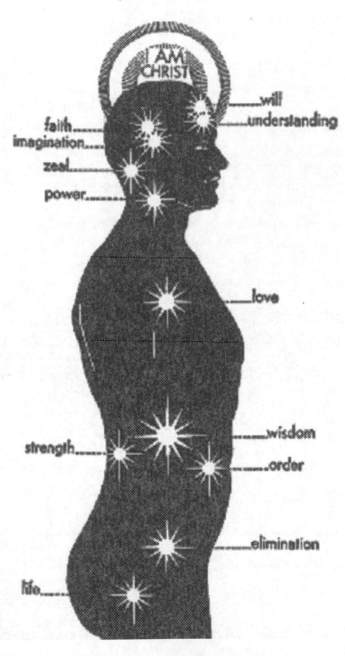

12 SPIRITUAL POWERS OF MIND TAUGHT BY JESUS & SYMBOLIZED AS OUR 12 DISCIPLES THAT WE NEED TO DEVELOP OUR GOD-CONSCIOUSNESS

1. FAITH – PETER - (dark blue) - center of head – is a masculine thinking power character trait, or faculty of our mind. Faith is our God-given ability to choose what we will believe; to choose our own ideas about God, our neighbor, and our purpose in life. If you believe in your own inner Spirit God guidance, then, you won't let outer ego-worldly beliefs or authorities make choices for you. Jesus helped Peter replace his false beliefs by changing to new God-Truth ideas and beliefs. "Faith is the substance of things hoped for, the evidence of things not seen." Faith envisions our God-given ideas, dreams and desires in our mind, and goes forth to express God's ideas into our outer physical world conditions.

2. SPIRITUAL PERCEPTION - STRENGTH – ANDREW – (green) – kidneys – This is a feminine feeling power faculty, or God-given character trait that comes from conscious daily prayer contact with our Father-Mind Mother-Love God. It is our power of knowing that God's Presence and Power dwells in us and all people, places and situations at all times. It is our sustained conviction that our God-Truth thoughts are stronger than our false fear based-thoughts and help us stand firm in our faith in God when the storms of life cross our path.

3. WISE JUDGMENT - JAMES – (yellow) – solar plexus – this is a feminine power faculty, or God-given character trait of righteous judgment. It is our ability to see beyond mere appearances, the love and Presence of God in all people, places and situations. God, the Master Mind-Love-Spirit, is forever teaching and guiding us in all our ways. We must all learn to let God work through us so we can judge righteously by seeing the good God within all.

4. LOVE – JOHN – (pink) – heart –back of stomach – this is an intuitive feeling faculty, the most powerful God-given feminine character trait. John symbolizes the embodiment of God's love incarnated in each and all of us. Love is the Spirit of God in action in us, for "We know that all things work together for good to those who express God's love, and are called according to His purpose." Rom. 8:28. It is experiencing the joy and ecstasy of fulfilling our oneness with God's boundless love-dream-purpose for us as sons or daughters of God. It is knowing that with love or "with God all things are possible to us who believe."

5. POWER OF OUR SPOKEN WORD – PHILIP – (purple) – larynx – back of the throat – this is a masculine thinking power faculty of our mind. He symbolizes the God-given power of our spoken word. As sons and daughters of God our words are the word of God, and whatever word we send forth into the world must fulfill what we send it to do in faith. Remember that we are one with God, the Universal Subconscious

Master-Mind-Love-Spirit, who takes our spoken word as law and creates for us what we think and say into our physical world.

6. CREATIVE IMAGINATION – BARTHOLOMEW / NATHANIEL – (blue) – back of head - this is a thinking faculty, or God-given mind power to creatively imagine and visualize, to see in our mind's eye, our God-given dream desires as already fulfilled and done "according to our faith." God gives us inspired dreams and visions for new creative possibilities of His will for us, to fulfill our heart's desires. This is what Jesus meant when he tells us, "Whatsoever you desire when you pray, believe you have already received it (see it in your mind as already done), and you have it." See your dream as already done and go forth. "You call Bartholomew to discipleship when you can imagine the reality of your fulfilled desire, and feel the joy of your answered prayer." said the great and loving metaphysician, divine science teacher, and writer Joseph Murphy.

7. SPIRITUAL UNDERSTANDING - THOMAS (gold) – forehead – this is both a thinking and feeling power disciple of our mind or spirit. At first Thomas was a doubter who believed only what his physical senses could reveal. He was 'double minded.' He believed in the material world more than the world of Spirit. Then he came to have faith in a Power greater than himself, and the Holy Spirit changed his thinking. He came to understand that the invisible world of mind or spiritual mental thought-ideas came from God which is the true cause source, and substance of all our ideas, dreams, and physical manifestations. With Thomas as your disciple you will know that God wills and works in you, as you.

8. WILL – MATTHEW – (silver) – forehead – this is the executive or intellectual thinking faculty, or character trait disciple common to all people. God has given us the free-will to choose what we will believe. Matthew means the executive decision making faculty of our mind. We decide what we will think, feel, and commit ourselves to fulfilling our God-given dreams, and God responds to our thoughts, words, and beliefs according to our faith. As we decide to let go of our false ego-centered self, and let God's will be done through us, we find we are never alone. We are strengthened in spirit, mind and body to fulfill our destiny, because Matthew means "given wholly unto God's will and desires for you."

9. ORDER - JAMES (Son of Alphaeus) - (olive green) – stomach – this is an intuitive, or feminine feeling faculty or character trait of order, or a tidy mind. When we allow only peace and love thoughts into our mind and heart kingdom, we find the same peace and love manifesting in our home, business, and all our relationships. This faculty is also called the power of your mind to discern or discriminate that we all live in a mental universe and that our negative beliefs are the cause of our physical diseases. So we pray to God to change our thoughts to positive truth beliefs so order, harmony and peace can return into our lives.

10. ZEAL – SIMON the Zealot – (orange) – back of the head - connects thinking and feeling faculties of our mind. Zeal is our spiritual mental power to go into action with enthusiasm, gusto, persistence, sticktuitiveness, tenacity, and the perseverance to achieve our God-given dream-goals and desires for good. "I spring forth with a mighty faith knowing I will be guided and given all I need," wrote Charles Fillmore the founder of Unity School. We know without doubt that our dream-desires come directly from God and we cannot fail to achieve our God-given vision-mission, for it is God's Spirit-Mind-Love working in us.

11. ELIMINATION/DENIAL – THADDEUS – (russet brown) - lower body – intuitive feeling faculty of our God-like mind to affirm only good thoughts from entering our mind kingdom and eliminating or denying entry to false fears and negative thoughts that separate us from others, such as, criticism, resentments, and condemnation. We have the God-given power to choose to deny, eliminate, and erase from our mind all error or evil thoughts, ideas and beliefs that have no substance, and to affirm only good God-Truth thoughts to rule our mind.

12. LIFE/REBIRTH – MATTHIAS - JUDAS - (red) –lower part of body – intuitive feeling faculty, or character trait of our God-given mind or spirit. Judas means your power to change your old negative ideas or former false ego-centered self and turn to God, a power greater than yourself, and experience a spiritual rebirth, and life transformation. We all, at some time in our life, experience the humbling of our false ego-centered self. I realize that my finite little ego-self is not God, and that "of myself I can do nothing;" just as Jesus said. I realize that my ego is powerless, and that I need a Power greater than myself to restore me to sanity. Judas represents our salvation from our smaller selfish ego-self by choosing to trust in God, the Universal Subconscious Master Mind-Love-Spirit who created us all, and "in whom we all live, and move, and have our being."

BREAKING FREE FROM THE PRISON OF OUR
FALSE EGO-CENTERED WORLD

Do not be afraid to express your thoughts and feelings today; for what you do and say are the foundation of what will materialize today and build upon for tomorrow. Most likely you will be met with opposition from within your ego-self, and without from outer authorities; but this is nothing to fear. Progress can only be achieved if you stick with your inner beliefs and what you know to be true in your heart, "for as you think in your heart (subconscious mind) so shall you be." - Proverbs 23:7

As a person I was living in a false egoistic consciousness and didn't know it. I was a know-it-all, full of vanity, pride, self love, and a false belief that I was God, and could do everything by myself. I believed that I didn't need anyone to help me achieve my material wealth and happiness. I was a person who was being totally codependent on others due to false beliefs, peer pressure, substances, inferiority, and inadequate doubts about myself.

These forms of the ego-self had no foundation to build upon a lasting mental loving comfort zone or a lasting material security and I was lost due to my ego and race world thinking. I had to admit to myself that I was in bondage to my own ego thinking and humbly asked for help from a Power or force higher and greater than myself, a God that controlled the universe. With this surrender and humbling of the ego we begin to realize the truth about the ego as a false self identity or lock, and we become aware of a new self identity of not being alone, but with an intuition that God is within us.

In asking for help for the first time, with our new God-awareness, we begin to see the power of prayer being answered, and that our Lord is greater than all the problems we may conceive. We also discover an inner sense of unity; that God's Presence and peace is within the subconscious mind of us all, and directing us in a good orderly direction.

This conscious contact with God begins to show us, now with a better understanding of the truth, where our prayers and thoughts come from, and that what rightfully belongs to us we will never lose if we learn to listen for the answer or solution from the creator of the universe within us. The most important message I learned was that I can only change my thoughts. I cannot change other people, situations or places. I have the power within to only change my creative formative thoughts.

This God-Power helped me change the way I saw myself from within. I was changed from an egotist concerned only with 'me, myself, and I,' into a new creation, a new inner-Spirit God-guided person that started to love, forgive and respect himself and others, and I felt the love and forgiveness of God in me. With this new acceptance of God and change of consciousness, I was able to discover-recover my true spiritual identity and spiritual mental faculties and powers, and learn the universal laws of mind, love and life that Jesus taught. I was able to show love and forgiveness to other people, and radiated love feelings towards them with no expectation of reward through my actions. God filled me with Love.

LOVE LESSONS TO REMEMBER

Our ego-centered finite mind is our false self. It is outer-authority-controlled, and under the illusion that it is God Almighty. It is the lie that leads us all to hell.

Of myself I can do nothing; but with God, the Universal Subconscious Master-Mind-Love-Spirit Force within me, all things are possible with good orderly direction. There is no separation from God, except ego-thinking makes it so.

The key that sets us free to be transformed and recover our true spiritual identity as sons and daughters of God is to admit through failure, suffering, and letting go of our ego-self persona - that without God we were powerless to manage our lives.

Spiritual identity is a knowing that God is within us and that we are in unity within God as a spiritual mental being having a human experience.

There is only One God, the Universal Subconscious Master-Mind-Spirit, and we are each individual expressions of a Loving Father-Mother God. This Truth sets us free.

Love is the most powerful of all of our faculties for it can override any power with its hunger for uniting our spirit, mind and body under One God-Mind-Love-Spirit.

By thinking only good positive thoughts and prayers for all people, we rise above all our egoistic vindictive emotions and separation ideas into unity and love for all.

We have the power to choose. We have options. We can let go of our false ego-self world of failure, fear, and self-pity, and choose to let God's inner Spirit guide us to spiritual love, true peace, creative expression, prosperity, happiness and freedom.

MEDITATION

(in U.S. Andersen's book "The Secret of Secrets")

I resign the dominion of the ego and surrender my life to God. I renounce the priority of sensual stimuli and find within my own nature the power to originate thought, feelings, and action. No longer do I exist as reflex to events around me, but now I take up the larger existence that descends from higher planes of mind and spirit.

I ally myself with the first cause, I identify myself with God. I make my life a living sacrifice to Him, surrendering each of my thoughts, feelings, and actions without desire for their fruits. No longer am I enamored of the vain desires of the ego. Fame and money and applause are not ends in themselves, and when sought as such are traps from which pain and suffering eventually ensue. I penetrate within myself to that core of consciousness that is pure being. There I take refuge, turning away from all strident demands of the beckoning surface ego-self, yielding my identity to God.

Yet I do not lose it. My "I" remains, is not engulfed, but now takes on greater awareness, and eternal significance. I expand outward from the centre of myself, beyond all horizons, beyond all limitations, seeking to include that which formerly included me, so that I may know God not only by penetrating Him but also by containing Him. Thus I am led to a mystic resolution of myself with the Divine, and He and I become one. By special deputation from above I am forthwith able to live a divine life upon earth. I seek not to change that which is ordained, but only to understand, to possess identical consciousness, to act in accordance with divine will, equal-souled to all results, existing always above the conflict, secure in the knowledge of union with God.

RECOMMENDED READINGS

1. The Sermon on the Mount, by Emmet Fox, Published by Harper and Row, 1934.

2. The Power of Your Subconscious Mind, by Joseph Murphy, Published by Prentice-Hall Inc., 1963.

3. Alcoholics Anonymous, by 100 Recovered Alcoholics, Published by Alcoholics Anonymous Worldwide Services, 1939.

4. Power Through Constructive Thinking, by Emmet Fox, Published by Harper and Brothers, 1932.

5. Lessons In Truth, by H. Emilie Cady, Published by Unity School of Christianity, 1946.

6. The Secret of Secrets, by U.S. Andersen, Published by Wilshire Book Company, 1958.

7. Three Magic Words, by U.S. Andersen, Published by Wilshire Book Company, 1954.

8. The Twelve Powers of Man, by Charles Fillmore, Published by Unity Books, 1930.

9. The Transforming System, by Jack Boland, Audio Tape Cassettes by Master Mind Publishing Company, 1986.

CHAPTER TWO

STEP CHOICE 2 FOR A CHANGE OF MIND & A LAW OF LIFE

We freely chose to believe or have faith that a loving God, a Power greater than ourselves, in whose Creative Universal Subconscious Master Mind or Spirit we all live and move and have our being, could restore us to sanity by uniting us in the fellowship of His Spirit-Mind-Love-Life in us all.

PRAYER CONNECTS OUR MIND WITH GOD'S INFINITE MIND!

"Whatsoever things you desire when you pray, believing you have already received them, you shall have them." – Jesus Christ in Mark 11:24

For many years, Ron, arrogantly thought his ego-self was God, and his small finite ego-world-mind knew it all. He thought he was self-sufficient unto himself, and didn't need the help or love of other people. With that kind of erroneous thinking and belief system, he progressed insanely alone into alcoholism for over twenty years. He lost everything he truly treasured in his life – his self-respect, integrity, his family, friends, business, honesty, peace of mind, and life purpose. Of his own inflated egoistic sick thinking and doing, he became bankrupt spiritually, mentally, emotionally and physically. At thirty nine years of age, he was a broken vessel. He had finally hit his bottom! There seemed to be no way out. He felt totally hopeless and a complete failure, because everything that he had built of his small finite ego-world-self had fallen apart. He felt utterly unlovable, damned and useless. He was so completely fear, guilt and shame-ridden, and so hopelessly alone because he had always worn many false masks to hide what he truly believed and felt about himself from others. What could he do? He felt totally lost and scattered. He was a walking dead man, a very lost soul. Everyone, it seemed, had abandoned him, and he felt unworthy of love. Where could he turn?

Where does a hopeless, broken and lost soul go? How could he be saved from this egoistic hell-hole he himself had created?

And then, the prodigal son, Ron, came to himself. Ron woke up and said to himself, "I will arise and go to my Father-God and tell him the truth:"Father, forgive me for I have sinned. I have wasted the inheritance you so graciously gave me in riotous living, and I have ended up alone, without you, in the pig pen of hell." For the first time in his life, Ron humbly chose to admit the truth that he had so painfully denied all those years; that of his own little finite ego-self he was powerless; that his whole life had become totally unmanageable, and that he needed help. He could not do it alone. He needed a Power greater than himself. So he humbly prayed, and asked God to save him from the delusional ego-self hell he had created. He remembered the Bible quote, "Anyone who calls upon the name of the Lord shall be saved," and "I am the resurrection and the life, you who believe in me though you were dead, yet shall you live." After that prayer of faith, miraculous events happened in Ron's life!

About a week after that prayer I, Ron, had a powerful life changing spiritual awakening experience that miraculously changed my heart, my mind, my attitudes, and my life forever. In a very real 4th dimensional dream state I saw myself standing on the top of a very high mountain, which symbolized the false ego-self-world I had created for twenty years, and I said to myself as I looked into the dark, bottomless abyss below, "God if you exist, catch me," as I stepped out in a leap of faith over the edge into the unknown. Immediately, I was being held very firmly and rocked lovingly in the arms of a figure I sensed to be Jesus, even though I couldn't see his face, and he spoke to me words I never thought possible. He said, "Ron, I love you just as you are, and you will never have to drink again to run away from yourself!" The very idea and feeling that I was loved, accepted, and forgiven, in spite of my horrendous past mistakes was overwhelming, for I truly believed that I was unworthy of love. Then, my whole past life flashed before my eyes like a motion picture, and I saw clearly how my own egoistic thoughts and arrogant prideful actions, and lack of love for others, had wounded and hurt so many people whose love I had taken for granted for so many years. As this happened, my water broke. The tears came and flooded my entire being. All the guilt and shame and fear-filled feelings I had dammed up within me over the past twenty years burst, and I wept profusely for the first time in my life. This loving visitation from God purified, cleansed and transformed my spirit, mind and body. I was never the same egoistic person again. God's loving Spirit was in me.

That December 8th day in 1979 I truly experienced an immaculate conception. I was reborn. My old ego-centered-worldly-self died that day, and I was resurrected into a new God-Presence or Cosmic God-Consciousness. Now, from personal experience, I knew the meaning of the Bible words, "I know that my redeemer lives,' and 'the old things, - my old ego-self - have passed away. Behold I make all things new!" This was my great humbling experience, the end of an old egoistic-world mental prison of bondage that had separated me from God, neighbor and all creation. "The Truth had set me free." It was the beginning of living in a new God-Consciousness, a new spiritual identity as a son of God; the beginning of a new life adventure and destiny, knowing I was loved and guided by a Loving Father or Master-Mind-Love-Spirit; that I would know peace and never be alone again! I had asked God to deliver me from all my hellish fears, and He had answered my prayer of faith, as I know He does with everyone who asks, for you cannot call upon the name of the Lord in vain!

The power of answered prayer by faith in God is witnessed daily all over the world.

People of all ages, all countries, and religions have believed in and testified to the miraculous healings and creative power of prayer. It is the spiritual solution to all our problems because God responds to all our prayers. And so we ask ourselves the fundamental question, "What is prayer?" Prayer is nothing less than our God-given power to communicate with and receive inspiration from God by direct conscious contact with Him, who dwells in the very heart or subconscious mind of each and all people as Infinite Intelligence and Boundless Love, whom Jesus called "our Father." We can never be separated from God except by our falsely thinking that we are.

HOW CAN I BE BORN AGAIN?

In letting go of my small egotistic-self, and coming to believe that every problem has a solution, by surrendering my thoughts and feelings to a Higher Power; by direct conscious contact with God through prayer and meditation; I came to have faith, trust, and love in God as the Universal Subconscious Master Mind-Love-Spirit who is in everyone and everything. There is no separation from God. "Our Father" is living within us and we are living within His One Universal and Infinite Divine Mind.

In order to achieve this state of consciousness we must be open minded, and willing to change our old negative beliefs to new thoughts or beliefs, because "we cannot put new wine into old bottles." In eliminating our old negative, destructive thoughts and replacing them with good God-thoughts into our subconscious mind, we are not leaving a void for negative thoughts to creep back into our thinking at a later date.

We come, by prayer and meditation, to realize that our subconscious mind thoughts and God's thoughts are one and the same. God, in our subconscious mind, always creates what our conscious mind thinks and believes, because It does not question the commands. It is when both our conscious and subconscious mind is in harmony, in the fourth dimensional state of God-Consciousness that only good can prevail, with positive results in our outer physical world. When only our ego-self-mind is in play, it is not aligned with God's Universal Subconscious Mind in thought or prayer. Then the results will be of a negative nature because of our disconnected and selfish ego-mind thinking or will power. This is teaching us the spiritual mental law of how our conscious and subconscious mind works, as well as, the spiritual mental law of humility; that we need surrender our small ego-self mind to God's Universal Subconscious Mind for peace.

The Power of Prayer fills our subconscious mind with good God-thoughts being re-affirmed by our conscious mind when we are in that fourth dimension of Spirit.   God is the Cause or Source of all our thoughts, desires and ideas, and the effects of our prayers is to know that it is God Himself who has placed them in our heart and mind kingdom so we can do His work through us in the outer physical world with love.   This is the Law of Life and Law of Belief that we must use in our day to day activities.   Your mind and mine are one with the Universal Master Mind-Love-Spirit of God.   All our thoughts or prayers are always answered in one form or another.   This shows us the spiritual mental Law of Supply and Demand, "Ask," said Jesus, "and believing you already have what you want, you shall receive, because "according to your faith, so is it done unto you!

HOW GOD SPIRITUALIZES OUR MIND THROUGH PRAYER

Prayer is practicing the Presence of God who dwells within the subconscious mind of each and all persons as Infinite Intelligence and Boundless Love Spirit.   We each have the power to make direct conscious contact with God, our Father-Mind Mother-Love Spirit within our heart and mind kingdom, which Jesus called our "Secret Place." Our mind is really the "city, house, or temple of God within us." We are one with God's Divine Master Mind or Spirit, and so God is the Source cause of all Substance, our thoughts, ideas, desires, dreams and manifestations whether we know it or not.   That is why the Scriptures of all creeds say that we are created in the image and likeness of God; that we are in Truth, all sons and daughters of God.   This is our true spiritual identity.   When we make direct conscious prayer contact with our Father-Mother God to answer our prayer requests and desires, we are always given inspirational ideas and solutions to our problems by the Master Mind Love Spirit.   What we need to understand is how our God-given mind works.   As we do this, we will learn how to use our God-given spiritual mental faculties or powers and laws of mind, and be empowered.

GOD CREATES THROUGH US BY LAWS OF MIND – CREATIVE THOUGHT-FAITH-IMAGERY

God creates by universal spiritual mental laws that apply to all persons at all times.

This is the good news that Jesus Christ, and many other sages and mystics, revealed to humanity through the centuries.   It is the great metaphysical law 'as within, so without." In other words, it simply means that we live in a mental universe that is owned and operated by a loving God.   One Divine Infinite Mind-Intelligence or Spirit, which indwells all creation, and in which all created things indwell.   Thus we, you and I, are all expressions of this One Divine Mind, which wants to individualize in us and as us.

God's Infinite Mind and Love Spirit dwells in our heart and mind kingdom, and is responsive to our prayer requests, thoughts and faith convictions by creating them into our physical world.   Whatever our conscious mind thoughts desire, and believe to be true, God creates according to the law of our faith belief which is a law of mind, a law of life, whether they be good or bad beliefs. "God is no respecter of persons," (Acts 10;34) and He responds to our conscious thoughts and faith convictions by creating them into physical form or manifestation. So we need to learn how to attune our finite conscious thoughts and beliefs with God's Infinite Master Mind thoughts and spiritual mental laws. This is the purpose of our daily prayer and meditation.

When we say we made a decision or choice to have faith in a greater Power than ourselves that could restore us to sanity, we are saying that we are willing to believe that there is a loving God, a Universal Infinite Master-Mind-Love-Spirit greater than ourselves, that we have been separated from in our false ego-mind, who can renew and restore our spirit, mind and body to its true identity, powers and sanity. Now let us review the following chart to help us better understand how our God-given mind works, so we can be inspired, enlightened and empowered to use our laws of mind.

HOW OUR CONSCIOUS & SUBCONSCIOUS MIND WORKS
AND HOW TO USE IT TO CREATE GOOD IN OUR LIVES

GOD – CREATIVE MASTER MIND-SPIRIT OF THE UNIVERSE

CREATIVE GOD MIND-SPIRIT-LOVE-LIFE-WORD-LAW

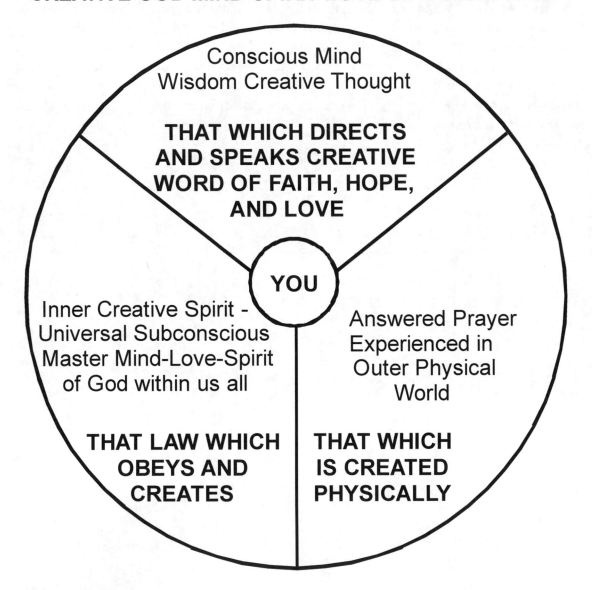

CREATIVE GOD MIND-SPIRIT-LOVE-LIFE-WORD-LAW

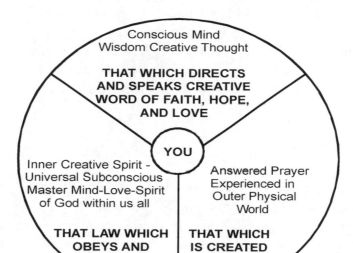

There is but One Universal Mind or Spirit; It is Omnipresent, All-Knowing and All-Powerful – It is all there is. Everything, visible and invisible is but a manifestation of this One Master-Mind-Spirit – the result of Its Creative Action and the becoming of that which It creates. Because you are made in the image and likeness of God, you can use your mind to choose thoughts, beliefs, and imagery by which you attract and bring good to you. Be aware of the Truth that everything is some aspect of God-Mind. Now examine the Creative Thought Process Diagram above and think of it as representing the entire universe. All of it is Divine Mind or Spirit. For the sake of clarity we divide it into three sections, but it is all One Divine Master Mind Love Spirit of the Universe!

Part 1 we call Conscious Mind. Automatically you think of your conscious mind as being that power faculty with which you think and plan. With it you become aware of ideas, thoughts, and desires. You analyze, make decisions, and carry on all mental processes. Let us think of it as the captain of a ship, who thinks of what is to be done and gives instructions to his crewmates. Needless to say, nothing could be accomplished if there were not some department heads to take those instructions and carry them out.

Part 2 is the part of Mind that obeys the directive words of Part 1. Think of it as a ship where the instructions are taken and carried out. We call this Subjective Mind, the Law which creates automatically according to instructions. It is your obedient Holy Servant to the commands of Part 1. Without Part 1 it would be useless for lack of instructions. Without Part 2, Part 1 would be helpless for want of something to give orders, and bring them to fulfillment. One part, therefore, is just as important as the other, and they need work together in harmony.

Look at Part 3 and realize that this is the only part of the universe you can experience with your physical senses - the realm of outer tangible things and conditions.   Here are the results of what was directed by Part 1, your inner Conscious Mind, and carried out by Part 2, God, the Universal Subconscious Master Mind.   Part 1 and Part 2 instigate and carry out; Part 3 is the result or effect.   In the diagram see the tiny portion called "You." Notice that you too, possess the three aspects of the Universal Master Mind; direction, creation, result.   After all you are gods, sons or daughters of God.

REMEMBER THIS!

1) Everything is and dwells in One Divine Universal Subconscious Infinite Master Mind and we are each and all part of It and the whole of It.
2) God's Universal Subconscious Master Mind responds to our conscious mind prayers, and creates out of Its Infinite Substance according to our thoughts, words, and faith convictions.
3) You have the right and power to choose what you will think and believe; therefore you may create good or negative conditions for yourself and others according to your thoughts and faith convictions or beliefs.
4) You control your own God Mind thought kingdom for good or evil, and can transform your life into an experience of happiness, health and prosperity and joy.   You have the God-given power of choice - to choose good or evil, or heaven or hell.   Pray to God to guide and direct your thoughts, desires, and destiny.

LOVE LESSONS TO REMEMBER

1. We all dwell in One Universal Intelligence, God, and that Master - Mind dwells in all created things as our Life and Love giving Spirit.
2. When we pray to our Father-Mother God within our subconscious mind, our Secret Place, we make conscious contact with our Creator.
3. As we surrender our false ego-self and listen to God's small still voice within us, we receive new inspired God-ideas, thoughts and direction.
4. Through prayer and meditation God helps us to replace negative fear thoughts with positive good God Truth thoughts and feelings.
5. We learn that what we truly think and believe in our conscious mind God, the Universal Subconscious Mind creates in our physical world.
6. Prayer is making direct conscious contact with God and asking Him for our daily needs and guidance.   Meditation is actively listening and receiving God's answer to solve our problems and do His will for us.

MEDITATION

(in U.S. Andersen's book " The Secret of Secrets")

I accept my body as a manifestation of Divine Mind or Spirit which created it. God's Spirit-Mind-Love-Life moves it and sustains it. I know this Universal Subconscious Intelligence to be greater than myself, to be an all-encompassing Divine Presence and Power that inhabits all creatures, and pervades the universe. My heart beats, my tissue lives in response to some perfect Order, some supreme harmony, some absolute power. I need not command the organs of my body to function properly. Health is mine, perfect function is mine by the simple surrender of my will to the Divine Will. Yet I recognize that the power of decision remains with me, for God has given me the free will that I may make my own choices, that I take a stand, choose a way, and that universal spiritual power will then lead me on the path that I have chosen. I, therefore assert, that I retain no hidden memories of pain in my subconscious. I bring up from the dim remembered depths of mind all those memories that prompt my subconscious feelings of hate, bitterness, anger, and fear. These negative emotions I choose to cast out of my life forever. By aligning myself with God, by identifying with His Master Mind-Spirit, by becoming one and equal-souled with all beings, I let go of all negative emotions and enshrine divine reason in their stead. Reason and attunement with God lead me down life's most hazardous paths with perfect composure and absolute surety. Because I attune my mind and heart with God my body functions in harmony with nature. There is perfect circulation and complete freedom. There is perfect elimination for there is absolute purpose. I follow the path of joy, for that is the road to attunement. I seek laughter, for in laughter all bonds disappear. I believe in the good ends of life and humanity, and this optimism rules my existence, strength, health and vigor.

RECOMMENDED READINGS

Sermon on the Mount, by Emmet Fox, Published by Harper and Row, 1934.

The Power of Your Subconscious Mind, by Joseph Murphy, Published by Prentice-Hall Inc., 1963.

Alcoholics Anonymous, by 100 Recovered Alcoholics, Published by Alcoholics Anonymous Worldwide Services, 1939.

Three Magic Words, by U.S. Andersen, Published by Wilshire Book Company, 1954.

The Secret of Secrets, by U.S. Andersen, Published by Wilshire Book Company,1958.

The Basic Ideas of Science of Mind, by Ernest Holmes and Willis H. Kinnear, Published by Science of Mind Publications, 1957.

CHAPTER THREE

STEP CHOICE 3 FOR SPIRITUAL FREEDOM IN GOD'S WILL

We chose or made the decision to turn our will and our lives over to the care of God, the Universal Subconscious Master Mind-Love-Spirit dwelling in the heart-mind kingdom of us all, to guide us in His will to our life purpose which is nothing less than our heart's desire to love and serve humanity.

GOD'S WILL FOR US IS TRULY OUR HEART'S DESIRE!

What does it mean to turn our will and our life over to the care of God? And what would lead a person to make such a decision? Many of us thought we were self-sufficient unto ourselves and were probably raised to believe that we didn't need anyone else to tell us what to think say or do. This seemed to work for quite some time, but eventually things fell apart and we were left all alone, broken, scattered, lost, and finally seeking answers to our problems that we could not face alone. Whether we bottomed-out from alcoholism, had a burn-out or nervous breakdown, or a mid-life crisis, whatever suffering it took, we finally came to the Truth that of our small finite ego-self of "me, myself and I," we could do nothing. Then, finally, we were ready to change our thinking and seek a Power greater than ourselves to help us. We woke up to the fact that a loving God, an Infinite Intelligence created us, and we were willing to turn our will and life over to Him to guide us in Truth.

There is an old truth saying, "God has a plan for every person and He has one for you." This makes sense when we realize that since God created us He has a definite plan for each and all of us. As we let go of our false ego-self, or 'edging God out mentality,' and let God's inner Spirit-Mind-Love-Life within our subconscious guide and direct us, we discover that God's will and purpose for our lives is nothing less than our heart's desire. As we start to listen and follow the still small voice of God stirring and calling us to do His will and service, it turns out to be everything that we would love to be, to do, and to have to make us happy, joyous, prosperous and free. We realize that God is our dream-giver and needs us to individualize and express His will and love through us and as us. So, when we turn our will and lives over to God's care, we are fulfilling His will, which turns out to be our heart's desire, to contribute our gifts and talents to the well-being and love of all humanity. God has given each of us a particular and unique love dream-vision and mission for our life and the talents and gifts to fulfill that God-given dream for the love and good of all. So, in Truth, as Jesus taught us, the most important thing you can do for yourself is to seek God's will for your life. The kingdom of God, and everything you need to fulfill God's will – in relationships, ideas, courage, moneys - will be provided for you, because 'it is your Father's great pleasure to give you His kingdom, to do His will."

DECLARATION OF OUR TRUE SPIRITUAL IDENTITY IN GOD

I AM a son or daughter of our Father and He spreads His grace in me and projects His love through me by the transformation and renewing of my mind. "He shall cover you with His feathers, and under His wings shall you trust: His truth shall be your shield and buckler." This means moving from a blind faith into an intuitive inner knowing that God's Mind is in me and all creation. "As within, so without." Faith means not conforming to our outer ego world-self, but listening instead to the inner voice of God within our subconscious mind. It is a knowing that even when we revert back sometimes into ego-consciousness that inner voice of God-Consciousness will prevail and guide our free will back on the right path. God changes us from within by changing our thoughts. Thus we don't make mistakes, but learn from the experience how to change our thinking. In listening to our subconscious God-Mind and having our conscious mind co-operate with His, we experience changes in our inner mental attitudes and our outer conditions by replacing our negative thoughts with positive thoughts. Faith in God is the golden key that unlocks the prison door of our false beliefs and attitudes, and sets us free to "right thinking" only good God-thoughts and truths.

Faith gives you a vision to follow; God, our Infinite Intelligence is creating the desires and thoughts that only you can do. With God as your Senior Partner and you as second in command, let your free will follow His inner-Spirit lead and give you the courage to overcome any problems that seem to stop you from fulfilling your dreams. You know that you are not alone, and understand who you are as a spiritual being in human form; a unity of spirit, mind, and body at one with God.

Faith is keeping in conscious contact with God on a daily basis to stay on the path of your desired dreams through prayer and meditation, or treatment, for new thoughts to proceed for the day. As Jesus said in the Lord's Prayer, "Our Father, give us our daily bread," Bread is our daily inspirational good God-thoughts, ideas and desires.

Faith in God is always growing in deeper understanding, and calling you to achieve new levels of God-Consciousness, for when we reach one goal God is planting new thoughts for us to dare to achieve so that we can fulfill His will or work through us.

With the previous two chapters and by applying this 12-Step process to our New Thought Spirituality Self-discovery-recovery treatment program we have now laid a solid foundation on which to build our new spiritual identity as sons and daughters of God, and how to achieve our God-given dreams or life purpose.

LOVE LESSONS TO REMEMBER

Faith is choosing to do God's will for us, which is nothing less than fulfilling our heart's desire, our God-given dreams and life purpose for the good and love of all.

Faith is intuitively knowing that God's Mind is within the subconscious of us all.

Faith is trusting our inner-Spirit and not conforming to outer ego-worldly ideas.

Faith is knowing that we are all spiritual beings having a human experience.

Faith is knowing that God's Universal Infinite Intelligence is responding to our creative thoughts and beliefs, our faith and prayer affirmations and suggestions.

Faith is knowing that God is our Senior Partner in all our life decision-making.

Faith is our new-found independence in depending solely on God as our guide.

Faith is trusting God and letting go of our false ego-self-reliance and self-sufficiency.

MEDITATION

(in U.S. Andersen's book "The Secret of Secrets")

All about me I see the infinite, eternal movement of God. In the surge of the sea, the flux of the tides, the precise patterns of the heavens, I see the purpose and presence of the Creator. He knows where He is going. All things, past, present, and future are apparent to Him. In His infinite wisdom He sees immediately the thing to be done and the perfect method of doing it. Therefore I turn over all my actions to Him. No longer will I be guided in my daily tasks by the willful promptings of my ego-self, but instead I turn inward to the very center of my being and listen for the voice and will of God. He is the master and the mover of my works. He is all that is, and I am being of His being and power, conscious only of Him. No more shall I hunger after the fruits of my labor. They belong to God, and I renounce all desire for them. I know that God never blunders, that He never is indifferent, and when it appears that I have failed in some immediate aim, I know it is only to prepare myself in the end for some rarer joy, some truer delight. I open myself to universal power and joy. I declare there is no limitation, no lack, no malfunction in my life.   A perfect power is governing all my affairs, pervading my very body.   I identify myself with that which is all-powerful, all-perfect.   I throw off the limitations, hurts, and frustrations of the finite ego.   In the depths of my being I am no longer a name, a past, a place.   I am pure spirit, infinite, eternal, all-encompassing.   That which I truly am, I can never cease to be.   I cast aside my ego-self and become my true Spirit-Self, host of the Indwelling God, in which I live in the light and love and mind or spirit of God.

RECOMMENDED READINGS

1. Power Through Constructive Thinking, by Emmet Fox, Published by Harper and Brothers, 1932.
2. The Power of Your Subconscious Mind, by Joseph Murphy, Published by Prentice-Hall, 1963.
3. The Secret of Secrets, by U.S. Andersen, Published by Wilshire Book Company, 1958.
4. The Sermon on the Mount, by Emmet Fox, Published by Harper and Brothers, 1932.

STAGE 2 CHOICES

THE DESERT EXPERIENCE: LEARNING HOW TO CONTROL OUR THOUGHT KINGDOM BY AFFIRMING GOOD AND DENYING ENTRY TO FALSE BELIEFS OR LIES

4-STAGE STEPS FOR SPIRITUAL SELF DISCOVERY-RECOVERY CHOICES OR CHANGES OF CONSCIOUSNESS FOR A NEW LIFE

Stage 2 Steps 4-5-6: By Changing Our Thoughts, We Change Our Life
We Choose Only Positive Thoughts to Enter our Mind & not Negatives

4)   We choose to make a searching and fearless moral inventory of
        ourselves, examine our conscience for Truth & errors ideas/acts.

   - We choose to let go of our fears, resentments, anger, control issues.

   - We choose to write down our fears, guilt, shame, and abuse issues.

5)   We choose to confess and admit to God, to ourselves, and another
        human being the exact nature of our wrongs.

   - We choose to ask God to face our secrets with a trusted person

   - We choose to accept God's love and forgiveness in order to be free.

6)   We choose to be entirely ready to have God remove all our defects
        of character and replace them with healthy character traits.

   - We choose to let God do for us what we cannot do for ourselves.

   - We choose to accept God's forgiveness of our past mistakes, and
     ask God to help us change our heart and mind beliefs for good.

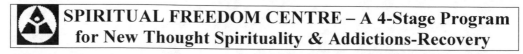

SPIRITUAL FREEDOM CENTRE – A 4-Stage Program for New Thought Spirituality & Addictions-Recovery

4-STAGE STEPS FOR SPIRITUAL SELF DISCOVERY-RECOVERY CHOICES OR CHANGES OF CONSCIOUSNESS FOR A NEW LIFE

<u>Stage 2 Choices: The Desert Experience: We Choose to Affirm Good and Deny Evil</u>
<u>The Thoughts We Sow In Our Mind-Heart Kingdom Will Reap Good or Bad Fruit</u>

1 Law of Individuality: God's Spirit-Mind-Love-Life is individualized in us all.
2 Law of Creative Thought: Inner thoughts-beliefs cause our outer experiences.
3 Law of Cause and Effect: We live in a mental universe: "As within, so without."
4 Law of Affirmation and Denial: We affirm Truth thoughts and deny false beliefs.
5 Law of Becoming Inner-Spirit guided and letting go of being outer authority led.
6 Law of the Lock and Seven Day Mental Diet to change our subconscious beliefs.
7 Law of Freedom of Co-dependency: We can only control our mind, not others.
8 Law of Mind: We have powers to think, believe, pray, imagine, love, and choose.
9 Law of Meditation-Receptivity: We ask, listen, and follow our inner God-guidance.
10 Law Of Forgiveness: God frees us from ego fears, limitation, sickness, and poverty.
11 Law of Creative Imagination: We pray, visualize-actualize God-ideas into form.
12 Law of Substitution: We choose to replace false beliefs with good God Truths.
13 Law of Attraction: Inner thoughts we believe with faith become outer realities.
14. Law of Will: We will to do God's will – Source of all good ideas-dreams-desires.

CHAPTER FOUR

STEP CHOICE 4: LEARNING HOW TO CONTROL OUR THOUGHTS

We chose to make a searching and fearless moral inventory of ourselves. By using a Seven Day Mental Diet, we learn how to affirm only good God-thoughts to enter our heart and mind kingdom, and to deny entry to negative false thoughts. In this way we are set free from the prison of our past false ego-self-thinking, and are transformed by the renewing of our mind by the creative God-given power of thought control.

THE NECESSITY OF MAKING A DAILY MENTAL INVENTORY

"As within, so without," means "As you sow in your mind, so do you reap."

The most important daily habit you can develop is to keep track of the thoughts you think and believe in, because what you think about all day long is what you become. Many of us are ignorant of this spiritual mental Truth which all great teachers like Jesus taught us. We are unaware that our inner thoughts and beliefs shape, mold, and create our outer physical world conditions. If we think negative thoughts, we in turn attract negative circumstances into our lives because we attract to ourselves the very thought energies that we send out. When we were kids our parents warned us "not to hang around with bad company," which meant kids that had a negative influence over our habitual thinking and behavior habits. Today, without knowing that our inner thoughts are creative, we allow negative thoughts like anger, resentment, criticism, ill-will, limitation, poverty, and sickness to occupy our inner mind kingdom. Then, we wonder why we attract those situations in our daily relationships with our families, associates and general life conditions.

So today, let's make a list of the thoughts we think, and feelings we feel on a daily basis, so that we can learn how to change our thoughts from within, and change our world from without.

This personal inventory of our daily thoughts will be the first step in helping us to change our lives for good because we have the God-given power to choose what we shall think, and feel, and be, and do. Let's remember the secret - "as within, so without."

YOUR BOOK OF LIFE IS WITHIN YOUR SUBCONSCIOUS MIND

"As you think in your heart (subconscious mind), so shall you be."
— Proverbs 23:7

The experience of traveling to that forbidden place of the mind, your subconscious mind,is the most scary and yet the most rewarding thing you could ever do in your life. It will set you free from the bondage of your self-centered ego-thoughts of separation from God and neighbor and all creation, to where you will be re-united with the power of God, the Universal Subconscious Master Mind within you and all. You will learn how to eliminate the false thoughts and beliefs that you believed in the past to be the real you. You will learn the universal spiritual mental law of belief; that you are the law of belief expressed, which means that your creative inner thoughts and beliefs shape your outer physical world around you. Thus, your subconscious thoughts and beliefs is your Book of Life.

The renewal of your mind comes in detaching from your false, negative ego-self thinking and connecting with God, the Universal Subconscious Master Mind within you. As you unite your finite conscious mind with your Father God's Infinite Master Mind within you as a Friend, He prunes your false ego-centered thoughts out, and turns the former desert of your false ego-mind thoughts into a garden of flowering new Spirit-led truth thoughts, which is your God-given inheritance, your spiritual mental powers and laws of mind.

A SEVEN DAY MENTAL DIET EXERCISE FOR THOUGHT CONTROL

"Be not conformed to this world, but be transformed
by the renewing of your mind." - Romans 12:2

You have the God-given power to choose to control and change your thinking, to change your thoughts, feelings and beliefs at any given time. As you change your inner thoughts and beliefs, your outer physical world will change accordingly. Many of us were quite ignorant, or unaware of the creative power of our thoughts, feelings and beliefs. So now we will learn how to use our God-given power to choose what conscious thoughts, feelings and beliefs we allow or let into our heart or subconscious mind kingdom by using a seven day mental diet exercise to control our thoughts, feelings and beliefs, or faith convictions.

This seven day mental diet exercise to allow and affirm only good God Truth thoughts and deny entry to negative false ego-thoughts to enter our heart and mind kingdom, or house, or city of God temple, will be difficult to do at first, but it will prove to be the greatest thing you have ever done. Starting today begin to stand back from your thoughts as an observer. Watch them come at you in unlimited supply, and wanting to enter into your heart and mind kingdom, the garden of your soul. Are they thoughts that are positive good God thoughts like love, peace, harmony, joy, prosperity or good-will towards others, or are they of a negative nature, destructive thoughts of anger, criticism, resentment, war, vanity, lies, limitation, inferiority and chaos that separate you from others? Now with God's help, who has given you the free-will power to choose your own thoughts, feelings and beliefs, choose to accept and affirm only good God thoughts and feelings and beliefs to enter your heart and mind kingdom, and choose to deny entry to any false negative mental poisons that are ego-centered and tend to separate you from God, your neighbor, and all creation.

Remember you are the watchman at the gate of your heart and mind kingdom. Your mind is like a city, a temple, and you are the king or queen who chooses which thoughts you will allow to enter, or deny entry into your heart and mind kingdom. God has given you dominion over your spiritual mental life and so "the conscious thoughts you sow in your subconscious mind are the harvest you will reap." As you do this inner mental diet exercise on a daily basis you will be amazed to discover how your outer life changes, as your inner thoughts change for the better. You will wake up to the fact or truth that "as your inner thoughts go, so does your outer life." Your thoughts have creative formative power to attract to you whatever you think and truly believe in, because we all live in God's One Divine Mind. This is called the universal spiritual mental law of attraction, and it always works according to the thoughts you think about and believe to be true all day long. So now you are aware that as you change your mental thoughts and beliefs, or faith convictions, you change your life because God, the Subconscious Mind creates for you exactly what your conscious mind directs it to do, "according to your faith in God working through you."

THE POWER OF DENIALS

The hardest thoughts and beliefs to prune or deny are the childhood beliefs that were taught to us by our parents and other outer authorities, especially religious ideas about who we are, who God is, and what we should believe, and do to have a happy life. These beliefs were imposed upon us when we were young impressionable children, who believed and accepted everything our loved ones told us to think and believe. Without a doubt, these childhood ideas and faith convictions have had a major impact on all of our lives. For example, the belief that there is a real place called hell, and that if we disobey our elder outer authorities, God will send us there to suffer for our mistakes is nothing less than a 'theological man-made error thought or belief' that has youngsters all over the world believing God is a punishing God. Many of us were also told that we had to toil by the sweat of our brow to make a living, and were born to be slave-servants to outer authorities who were created to be our lords and masters; and that all our sickness, pain, poverty, death, and other limitations was God's will for us. False beliefs lead to slavery and Truth beliefs lead to spiritual freedom, and we have the power to choose to affirm life and deny death or evil.

Today, as adults, many of us continue to live by those same childhood ideas and beliefs, and don't know that we have the power to choose our own thoughts, desires, dreams, and beliefs. That is why Jesus, our Master Teacher, told us to "let go or deny our father and mother's beliefs and choose to follow our own inner-Spirit guided beliefs, and follow our own soul's integrity." Denial is our God-given power to choose, to let go of, or not give reality to any and all false negative, destructive ideas or beliefs or situations of our past that were not true, and replace them with affirmative truth beliefs that set us free.

So let us now freely choose to no longer be conformed to this world, or to the opinions of outer authorities, whether it be our parents, religious teachers, the media, or our peer groups and allow their ideas and opinions and beliefs to control our mind, thinking and feeling nature. Rather, let us begin right now to go within our heart and mind where God dwells, in our Secret Place as Jesus called it, and listen and follow God's inner-Spirit guidance and intelligence within our own heart or subconscious mind to help us rebuild our own life by choosing to change our heart and mind kingdom. As we choose to affirm only good God thoughts, feelings and beliefs, and deny entry to false ego-centered lies, our entire life will be transformed by the renewing of our mind. This is the great law of mind or life common to all people worldwide, "as within, so without." So, guided by God, we will know a new spiritual mental freedom and a new happiness.

In using this God-given power of denial, we freely choose to affirm four new truths to live by day by day. First, we affirm that there is no reality to evil, or the devil, or hell, and that they are illusions that we create through our own thinking and believing. Second, we affirm that there is no absence of life, substance or intelligence anywhere in the universe, for God is all these and only good. Thirdly, we deny the belief that there is a power called the devil or evil, which has equal power and opposes Good or God. We affirm that there is only One God which is Good. Otherwise, there would be chaos instead of a Universe of Order. Fourth, another thought or belief we choose to deny as truth, is that there is no real pain, sickness, poverty, old age, fear and death, unless we choose to think and believe them to be real by creating them in our own mind. Shakespeare wisely noted this truth when he said, "There is no good or bad, but thinking makes it so." Therefore, I choose to think and believe that there is nothing in the entire universe for me or us to fear, for there is no fear in a God of Love. There is only health, harmony, peace, prosperity, joy, and abundant life. As we practice these denials daily, we must not leave a void, but rather replace them with positive truth thoughts, feelings, and faith affirmations and actions. If a void is left open in our heart and mind kingdom, the negative beliefs will return because there is nothing to replace them. So let us use our God-given power to choose to deny evil and affirm only good. This is called the spiritual mental Law of Substitution.

THE POWER OF AFFIRMATIONS

"It is done unto you according to your faith."

So, we now accept the God-given dreams and desires of our heart, and we now know that "with God all things are possible to us." We now learn how to use our God-given spiritual mental power of affirmation. We have the God-power to choose to affirm, and let into our heart and mind kingdom only positive truth thoughts by realizing that God's Universal Subconscious Master-Mind-Love-Spirit is love, intelligence, substance, omnipresence, omniscience and omnipotent life within us and all creation. Here's a prayer prescription for you and four truth affirmations.

Say this prayer affirmation, "First, I now affirm and accept the Truth, that I am a child or individual manifestation of God, and that all the power of our Father-Mind Mother-Love God flows through me and all creation. Second, I now affirm and accept that I and all creation are a part of God, and One with His Holy Spirit-Mind-Love-Life in each and all of us. Thirdly, I now affirm and accept the Truth that I am a spiritual being in perfect harmony with our Father-Mother God, and that nothing can ever hurt me, or harm me, or make me afraid. And last but not least of these major Truth affirmations, I affirm that it is God who works in me to will and to do whatever He wishes me to do, and God and I are a majority and cannot fail."

By doing and practicing this power of denial and affirmation on a daily basis, we are starting to use and practice our God-given spiritual mental powers and laws of mind. Especially the Law of Unity, the transformation of our false, negative ego-self consciousness into the truths of God-Consciousness, into a mind set of being at one and attuned with God, our Father, Infinite Intelligence and Mother, Boundless Love Spirit. This changing of our thinking, or consciousness, gives us the spiritual mental freedom to affirm and accept our true spiritual identity as sons or daughters of God, who are created and formed by His hands. As we claim our new spiritual identity, we claim our freedom from co-dependency on outer people, situations, and outer authorities; and we claim our God-given power to choose and change our own thoughts with His inner-Spirit-guidance by eliminating and letting go of the false beliefs, lies, and illusions that have no foundations to build upon. By changing our inner thoughts, feelings, and beliefs through our God-given powers of denial and affirmation, we start to see changes in our outer physical life conditions and environment for the better. This process, of learning to control our heart and mind kingdom, reveals to us our God-given power of creative thought, and the law of cause and effect as universal spiritual laws of mind. Now we understand better the true meaning of "As you think in your heart - subconscious mind - so shall you be."

LOVE LESSONS TO REMEMBER

Your finite ego-self is your false-self identity. You really are a son or daughter of God!

You have control over only one thing, your own thoughts, "As within, so without."

We all have the God-given spiritual mental power to choose to affirm only good God thoughts, and deny evil, or negative vindictive thoughts to enter our mind kingdom.

It is the knowing that God's Universal Subconscious Mind or Spirit guides my will, beliefs, and actions with love and understanding that sets me and all people free.

I intuitively know that as my finite conscious mind unites with God's Infinite Mind and Boundless Love I am always living under the law of love and abundant life.

I know that through daily prayer and meditation God dwells in me and I live in God-Consciousness as a spiritual being in human form. "I and my Father are one."

By thinking and affirming only positive good God-thoughts and feelings towards all people, I eliminate my vindictive emotions and thoughts, and unite in thought, peace and harmony with all my brothers and sisters worldwide.

Your subconscious mind is your Book of Life. What you truly think and believe with faith within your inner mind or heart kingdom, God creates in your outer physical world. The Truth is: "the good or bad thoughts you sow in mind, so shall you reap."

We live in a mental universe, and in order to change our life, we must change our inner thoughts from within. Our thoughts are the only mover, and God is the only Creator. God, the Universal Subconscious Mind creates what we think and believe to be true. Thought + Faith = Creates. Learn how to use and control your inner thoughts!

MEDITATION

(in U.S. Andersen's book "The Secret of Secrets")

There is a power within me which I can use to overcome all obstacles, solve all problems, a power that flows from the farthest reaches of the universe, out of the infinite, omnipotent mind of God. I give over my work, its progress and path, to Him. Only He knows the real purpose and actual nature of the things I do and the goals I aspire to achieve. Only He can chart a perfect course to the destined shore. No longer do I allow my finite and false ego-self to direct my life and work, for in such egoistic blindness there is only suffering. It is knowledge I seek, and joy, and I find them through serving the Divine Master Mind. No matter the negations I encounter, I see beyond them, perceive their other face. All serve a purpose, each is a step in spiritual soul development and each may be overcome by an inner perception that springs abundance out of lack, expansion out of limitation, success out of failure, victory out of defeat. I know that God is all things at all times; therefore I affirm the positive. By divine alchemy I call forth good from evil, not because I will it, but because I perceive it, because I know that God reveals to the individual soul that which his consciousness is able to perceive. My God-Consciousness surpasses the limitations of my ego-self, soars out to encompass all beings, and all life. I affirm my knowledge of God's manifold expression, and I accept only good as befits my spiritual stature. Success is mine, true place, victory, progress, abundance, and joy.

RECOMMENDED READINGS

1. Power Through Constructive Thinking, by Emmet Fox, Published by Harper and Brothers, 1932.
2. Lessons in Truth, by H. Emilie Cady, Published by Unity School of Christianity, 1946.
3. Three Magic Words, by U.S. Andersen, Published by Wilshire Book Company, 1954.
4. The Secret of Secrets, by U.S. Andersen, Published by Wilshire Book Company, 1958.
5. How To Use the Laws of Mind, by Joseph Murphy, Published by DeVorss & Company, 1980.

CHAPTER FIVE

STEP CHOICE 5 FOR SPIRITUAL SELF-DISCOVERY-RECOVERY

We chose to admit to God, to ourselves, and to another human being the exact truth of our past negative thinking ego-fears and attitudes, and let them go by becoming inner-Spirit-directed, and recovering our true spiritual self identity by letting God renew and restore our mind, thoughts, beliefs, and our entire life.

COMING OUT OF THE SHADOWS INTO THE LIGHT

"The Truth will set you free … and everyone else too."

Unless we admit our mistakes we cannot change. We need to have the courage of not only facing ourselves, but the courage to be honest in telling another person our deepest fears, misdeeds and feelings. This is not a state of humiliating yourself but a state of being humble in rising out of the ego-consciousness into the spiritual God-Consciousness of freedom. If neglected, it will keep us in bondage to lies, false ego, limitations, lack, negativity and the selling of your very soul or true self integrity.

The courage to take this step action is a choice that comes from within yourself knowing that you are being freed by God from unwanted burdens of the past that are not meant for you to carry. This step choice of being totally honest with ourselves by confessing our truth is common in all religions and spiritual growth groups throughout the world. Sharing honestly with another person brings the truth light into the darkness of our dark secrets. It reveals and releases the false masks and hidden fears of our ego-consciousness with a new spiritual awakening and identity. By sharing our story we find out that we are no different or worse than other people, it was just our ego-consciousness generating those fears so that we would remain subservient to them.   What a freedom to know we can make our free conscious choices with the help of God's Subconscious Mind within us!

In admitting our truths by using our God-Consciousness we learn that God is only good and supports and guides us in giving us the courage to express our truths without the fear of resentment or the opinions of other people.   God's inner Spirit guidance will direct the choice of words we use in confessing our mistakes and as we follow this inner inspiration we know that we are never alone and always God-guided.   Once we have learned let go and let God lead us to our true spiritual-self identity and powers of mind, we are free to share our deepest secrets with other persons we trust without the fears, reservations and limitations of our false ego-centered consciousness.

CONFESSION IS AN 'INSIDE JOB' THAT SETS YOUR SOUL FREE

"To your own self be true, then, you cannot be false to anyone."

Confession is good for the soul – Unless we admit our mistakes and let go of our old, false ego-centered ideas, or 'stinking thinking' beliefs and consequential behaviors, we cannot change or grow into a new state of consciousness; into a new person, the son or daughter God intended us to be.   As William Shakespeare said, "To your own self be true, and then it follows as the night the day, you cannot then be false to anyone." So we find that telling the truth about ourselves, by admitting our mistakes, our false inner thoughts, feelings, beliefs and behaviors, is the key to spiritual freedom.   It is an 'inside job,' that only you can choose to take to save your soul.   "What does it profit a man if he gains the whole world, but loses his soul," said Jesus.

Sharing our true thoughts, feelings and mistakes with others honestly and truthfully helps us heal not only ourselves but others by our example for the common welfare of all.   It helps us to see clearly that we need to be willing to change our thinking and feelings or heart, (subconscious mind) from within, in order to change our outer life conditions and environment. It is always an 'inside job,' for "as we think and feel and believe with faith in our subconscious mind or heart, so shall we be." The wonderful metaphysical law of the universe is the truth that … "As within, so without."

We need to come out of the darkness of error thinking and feelings.   We need to let go of our false ego-masks, and the lies of our fear, guilt and shame-based ego-self beliefs, and the 'dark night of our soul separation from God.' As we let in the light of good God ideas, thoughts, truths and laws of mind, we can honestly experience our true spiritual identity and God-given spiritual mental powers as a son or daughter of God.

DISCOVERING THE KINGDOM OF GOD'S MIND IS WITHIN YOU

"The kingdom of God is within you – you are gods, all sons and daughters"

This step choice we make of confessing our mistakes or error thinking and being willing to change and grow by being honest and truthful with God, ourselves and another person requires the courage we ask for in prayer and meditation, and receive, from God's Spirit-Mind-Love-Life dwelling in us all. It is a spiritual universal law that was taught by all spiritual teachers like Jesus through the ages. It is absolutely essential to spiritual self- discovery, and if neglected, will keep a person in bondage to the lies of their false ego-self identity which leads to negativity, lack, limitation, inadequacy, powerlessness, and eventually a living death, for it is the selling of your soul to false ego-idols and gods.

The power of sharing our story with others sets us free from bondage to our outer directed small ego-centered world consciousness, and helps us rise up into Cosmic God-Consciousness where we are never alone and always united with God's Divine Mind-Spirit-Love-Life, the Source of all our creative ideas, desires, dreams, thoughts, feelings, and power. Is it any wonder that Jesus says to us all, no matter what our religion, creed, color, or sex may be, "the kingdom of God is within you." Let us then choose to discover our true spiritual identity and spiritual mental powers, and learn how to use our God-given spiritual laws of mind, love and life to fulfill our God-given dreams and unique calling to love and serve all humanity and glorify our Father-Mother God in the doing of His Holy Will and purpose for our individual and collective well-being. Let us choose to let go of our small and false ego-centered identity and put on the Mind or Love Spirit of our Father-Mother God-Consciousness that was in Christ Jesus.

Remember who you are, your true identity. "You are gods, sons and daughters of the Most High." Therefore, now that you have freely chosen to let God be your Senior Life Partner, you realize that "with God all things are possible to you," for you intuitively know that it is God who thinks, wills and acts in and through you, and as you. We are all individualized expressions of the One Divine Mind and Love Spirit of the universe, and all power is given us who claim it. Glory be to God in whose image and likeness we are all created, and in whom we all live, move, and have our being. "Now is the acceptable time of the Lord." Let us each claim our God-given spiritual mental powers and inheritance as a son or daughter of God.

LOVE LESSONS TO REMEMBER

We are never alone in sharing the truths about ourselves to another person for God guides and wants us to tell the Truth and be free of hidden fears that were just false lies.

Our true spiritual identity sets us free from the bondage of our past false ego-self identity.

By turning to God's Divine Subconscious Mind kingdom within us we discover our true spiritual identity and powers as sons and daughters of God and we come into the Light.

As we listen to God's still small voice within us we become inner-Spirit guided and speak only words of truth that set us free from our past outer-authority negative ego-self beliefs.

As God helps us learn to love and respect ourselves, we in turn do the same for others.

We now live knowing that our Father-Mother God is in us all, and we are never alone again.

"The kingdom of God is within you" means that God's Divine Mind-Spirit is within us all.

"To thine own self be true, and it follows as the day the night, you cannot then be false to anyone," said William Shakespeare. Let God's Truth guide your heart-mind kingdom.

"The Truth will set you free," said Jesus, "and it turns out it sets everyone else free too.

MEDITATION

In admitting my erroneous masks of ego-consciousness and actions and sharing my inner conscious thoughts with God, He gives me new life and understanding, and courage to share my past experiences and beliefs with another person. This revealing truth sets me free of the bondage of ego-self and confirms God's Presence working in me. This coming out of the shadows of ego-self into the light of God's love gives me strength to go forth to fulfill my life through the power of God. The false ego-beliefs of past limitations, fears and negative thinking no longer have power over me. My mind, heart and body are free and are in harmony with God-Consciousness. I am a spiritual being, a son or daughter of God. I am part of and an individualized expression of the Divine Presence in me and all.

As my finite ego-mind unites with God's Universal Subconscious Master Mind I am purged of past fears, and misdeeds; and past negative thinking is replaced by God-thoughts which rebuild my life on a foundation of love, trust, and faith. These radiate outward to all the world, and I become a new God-Conscious person. The words of Scripture are fulfilled in me, for "the old (life) has passed away … Behold I make all things new!"

RECOMMENDED READINGS

Sermon on the Mount, by Emmet Fox, Published by Harper & Row, 1934

Three Magic Words, by U.S. Andersen, Published by Wilshire Book Company, 1954

The Power of Your Subconscious Mind, by Joseph Murphy, Published by Prentice-Hall, Inc., 1963

CHAPTER SIX

STEP CHOICE 6: HOW TO USE YOUR CREATIVE IMAGINATION

We chose to be entirely ready and willing to have God remove all our negative character defects; to change our thinking from ego to God-Consciousness; and to inspire, enlighten, and empower us to use our spiritual mental faculties and laws of mind to fulfill His will and God-given dreams for us for the love of all humanity.

PRAYER & MEDITATION IN GOD'S PRESENCE MEANS GOD'S SPIRIT-MIND-LOVE-LIFE CHANGES US FROM WITHIN

When we wake up to the Truth that "we all live, and move, and have our being in One God, the Universal Subconscious Master-Mind-Love-Spirit, which yearns to individualize in each and all of us; and that our Father-Mother God is only good; and is Everywhere Present, All-Knowing, and All-Powerful, we better understand why it is so important that we willingly choose to pray and meditate and live in God's Presence, Peace and Power at all times. God helps us let go of our false ego-self and proceeds to shape and mold us into His image and likeness. God guides us to do His will and fulfill our God-given dreams to love and serve all humanity.

One of the most powerful prayers we can use in surrendering our false ego-self and consecrating our lives to God's love can be found in chapter six of the big book "Alcoholics Anonymous" which says, "My Creator, I am now willing that you should have all of me, good and bad. I pray that you now remove from me every single defect of character which stands in the way of my usefulness to you and my fellows. Grant me strength, as I go out from here, to do your bidding." As we turn over our fears, doubts, and negative thinking to Him, we take on a new identity as a son or daughter of God. As we pray to God in our heart and mind kingdom and listen to His inner-Spirit-guidance; we receive inspirational ideas or thoughts to solve our problems; we think only good God-thoughts, words and deeds; and our life purpose is revealed to us.   This is the spiritual freedom we have sought and hungered for all our lives, knowing that God is in us and we are never alone.

Daily prayer and meditation or practicing the Presence of God in us, helps us awaken to the truth, that the universe is owned and operated by a loving God who seeks to individualize and express Himself through each and all of us for the good of all. As we learn to let go and let God govern our thinking and feeling nature, and guide us in doing His will, which is nothing less than our heart's desire, we unite our soul or conscious mind with God's Universal Subconscious Mind-Spirit within our heart and mind kingdom.   It is God who works in us to renew and transform our entire lives, our thinking, our thoughts, ideas, desires, attitudes, and beliefs.   Our finite ego-self can't do this alone.   So with faith and courage we let go and let God.

HOW TO IMPLEMENT OUR PRAYER THOUGHTS & DREAMS

"It is God at work in you, giving you the dream, the will,
and the power to achieve His purpose."
Philippians 2:13

The whole of our outer physical life experiences comes from the inner thoughts and faith convictions we feed our subconscious mind and which we accept as truth.   As we let go of our ego-self-conscious shortcomings, and let God work in us through daily prayer and meditation, we discover that our dreams and desires in life are one and the same with God's, because it is He, not our ego-self, who has planted them in our heart and mind.   It is when our conscious mind and God's Universal Subconscious Mind within us are in unison that we learn that we are not separate, but One and All-Powerful.

This is teaching us that our God-given power of creative thought or prayer power is greater than what our ego-self could ever desire or dream of thinking or putting into action.   For all our desires are God-given dreams for us to achieve and to fulfill our lives.   In this fourth dimensional God-Consciousness of being one with our Creator, we come to see that the process of fulfilling our dreams operates in a circle of prayer steps, that revolve around each other in a very harmonious relationship, to manifest our dreams in the physical world.   We will study this process in our next chapter.

"All things work together for good to those who love God
and are called according to His purpose."
Romans 8:28

All our dreams are really God-given and they represent God's will for us to have a loving, happy, joyous, prosperous, and free life.   They are our deepest thoughts or desires to do or fulfill a need that was planted into our conscious mind by God, the Universal Subconscious Mind, and these dreams have no barriers or limitations unless we impose them by our own negative thinking and false beliefs.   It is up to us to decide if we want to choose to do and accept our God-given dreams as true, or think it is nothing less than idle wishful ego-thinking. If it is false then discharge it from your mind.   In deciding to accept our God-given dreams and desires we must have a loving feeling and faith that we can do it to completion because we know God is in us and all, and that we are not alone.   With God's inner-Spirit guidance in us, we make a plan in faith of how to go ahead, and write it down on paper to impress it into our subconscious mind.   Your dream-plan always implies that it is your purpose to fulfill God's will for you, and the confirmation of your free will to work in and through Him in achieving your dreams.   God always provides us with a love vision to see, faith to believe, and the courage to do, for a man, woman, or nation without a love-dream-vision-mission grows old in spirit, lives a purposeless life and will perish.

USING OUR GOD-GIVEN POWER OF CREATIVE IMAGINATION

"God has a plan for every person and He has one tailor-made for you."

God created each and every one of us with a purpose and He has placed that desire or dream within the heart and mind of each of us through the power of our God-given creative imagination.   Each and all of us have unique gifts and talents that are needed for us to contribute to the well-being of all humanity, and as we discover God's will for us, our love dream purpose in life, we find it is nothing less than our heart's desire, what we would love to be and do with our lives that would bless all.

It is through our creative imagination that God's Universal Subconscious Mind speaks to us.   Through prayer and meditation we ask ourselves, "What can I creatively imagine that I would love to do, and that would contribute to the well-being of all my brothers and sisters, and that would at the same time make me happy, joyous, prosperous and free? That is precisely what God is calling you to be and do and have when you listen and respond to His still, small voice within your very heart or subconscious mind.   This is the reason and purpose God created you and every person who has ever, or will ever live.   Now you understand why you and I need to pray and meditate to discover our heart's desire or true life purpose, our God-given love dream, vision mission in life, because it is God's will and purpose for you, and me and all, and we can never be happy until we find our God-given dream.

We all ask ourselves at one time or another, "What can I personally do to contribute and make this world a better place for all humanity? What love-dream-vision-mission has God placed in my heart for me to do?" My own quest to answer this question came many years ago when God called and gave me the love-dream-vision mission to teach His New Thought Spirituality and Science of Mind principles.   This helps people better understand the common and universal step-choices to spiritual self-discovery-recovery that are necessary to all people who, like myself, have lost their path through various addictions. God guided me in this quest by leading me to study and practice His God-given laws of mind and develop a unique one year spiritual growth program to help people become inner-Spirit guided. With this program they can all learn how to use their spiritual mental faculties of creative love, faith, thought, imagination, word power, will, understanding, and success, in order to inspire, enlighten, and empower people everywhere to claim their God-given spiritual identity and powers, and live loving, fulfilling lives as sons and daughters of God. This is the love-dream vision God has given me and my dear friend Eric in writing this book and sharing our spiritual program for the good of all people worldwide. We are now in the process of training others who are called by God to do this same work; and who will set up branch offices to teach God's New Thought Spirituality and science of mind, or addictions-recovery spiritual program to all people in all countries worldwide.

LOVE LESSONS TO REMEMBER

Our inner thoughts create our outer physical life conditions because we live in a mental universe in which we are all One in God's Universal Subconscious Mind.

Prayer and meditation is how we make direct conscious contact with our Father-Mother God, the Universal Subconscious Mind or Intelligence within all humanity.

God has an individualized love dream-vision-mission plan for each and all persons, and He has one tailor-made for you. Your job in life is to discover God's will or love purpose for you, your true place that will fulfill your heart's desire and life purpose.

You have all the God-given spiritual mental powers and laws of mind within you, and you must learn how to use them, in order to fulfill your love-dream-desires for the good and love of all humanity.

When you let go of ego and let God's Spirit-Mind-Love-Life individualize and work through you, you'll understand what Henry Thoreau discovered, "if you advance confidently in the direction of your God-given love-dream-vision, and endeavor to live the life you have imagined in your heart, you'll meet with a success unheard of in common hours." It is your God-given birthright and your passport to success.

MEDITATION

(in U.S. Andersen's book "The Secret of Secrets)

I acknowledge the existence of the Divine, and I dedicate my life to Him. I focus my mind on God each waking moment, seeking His Presence, longing to know Him. All that

I am, my work, my thoughts, my very being, I consecrate to the Divine. In Him I have my existence. I see His hand in every flower, bush, tree, and created thing; the warmth of His Presence is everywhere. Into whatever dangers I go, by whatever roads I travel, He is there. He is my Comforter and Guide. I surrender my life to Him, forsake my ego-self, and take refuge in the Supreme. No longer will I struggle with the events and forces of the world. I accept them; see them as the divine will working out the thing that needs to be done. I join forces with God by surrendering to Him my human hopes and dreams. I attain ascendancy over my mental and material mind, over my individual ego, by making a sacrifice of all my works, my goals, my thoughts and dreams. I see that all of life is a sacrifice to the Divine. Through all the confusion and struggle of ego against ego, He works serenely toward His ultimate purpose. Nothing is lost, nothing destroyed, for in reality there is nothing but God. Upon the altar of His Presence I lay my action, thoughts, emotions, and my will. By consecration, surrender, and sacrifice of my personal will and vanity, I enter into a state of pure adoration for God who is true and eternal. Love grows in me as a ruling passion of life, for it is my longing to be re-united with my universal Self. I know all things by my oneness with them. They are me; I am they. We are fused, united, bound together by Divine Love as equal-souls.

With the completion of this chapter on Step Choice 6 we leave our Stage 2 spiritual self discovery-recovery process of learning the techniques and methods of how to use our God-given power of choice to affirm good and deny evil to control our heart and mind kingdom, and we are now ready to launch into a new Stage 3 state of mind or consciousness, the Resurrection Experience, in which we will learn how to claim our God-given spiritual mental powers and laws of mind by applying and living in the 12-Steps of the Circle of Prayer, and how to heal all our relationships for peace and good-will in our lives.

RECOMMENDED READINGS

Lessons in Truth, H. Emilie Cady, published by Unity Books, 1954.

Alcoholics Anonymous, Published by Alcoholics Anonymous World Services, Inc. 2004.

Three Magic Words, by U.S. Andersen, Published by Wilshire Book Company, 1954.

The Secret of Secrets, by U.S. Andersen, Published by Wilshire Book Company, 1958.

The Power of Your Subconscious Mind, by Joseph Murphy, Published by Prentice-Hall, Inc., 1963

THE RESURRECTION EXPERIENCE: CLAIMING & USING OUR GOD-GIVEN SPIRITUAL - MENTAL POWERS AND LAWS OF MIND

**STAGE 3 STEPS FOR SPIRITUAL SELF DISCOVERY-RECOVERY
CHOICES OR CHANGES OF CONSCIOUSNESS FOR A NEW LIFE**

<u>Stage 3 Steps 7- 8- 9:</u> Becoming Aware We Seek Peace with God,
<u>Ourselves, and Neighbors</u>
<u>Practicing the Spiritual-Mental Character Traits & Laws of Love,</u>
<u>Forgiveness, Truth, Patience, and Tolerance</u>

7)   We humbly choose to ask God to remove all our shortcomings.

  -   We choose to let God guide and direct our thoughts, words, deeds.

  -   We choose to pray daily for love, peace, patience, and tolerance.

8)   We choose to make a list of all persons we have harmed and
      become willing to make amends to all of them.

  -   We choose to accept God's forgiveness and forgive all who hurt
     us.

  -   We choose to deal with and clean up the wreckage of our past.

9)   We choose to make direct amends to people wherever possible,
      except when to do so, would injure them or others.

  -   We choose to admit our errors and asked others to forgive us.

  -   We choose to thank God for healing our relationships with peace.

STAGE 3 CHOICES TO DEVELOP OUR SPIRITUAL CHARACTER TRAITS & USE THE LAWS OF MIND TO FULFILL OUR DREAMS

<u>Stage 3 Choices: The Creative Resurrection Experience: Claiming Our God-Powers</u>
<u>We Learn How to Use the 12 Steps of the Circle of Prayer and Make Our Dreams Come True.</u>

1 Law of Spiritual-Mental Healing: Put on the mind of God and speak the word.
2 Law of Spiritual Individual Identity: You are a unique son or daughter of God.
3 Law of Living in the Circle of Prayer to fulfill God's will and dream purpose for us.
4 Law of Forgiveness: We forgive others as God has forgiven us and set us free.
5 Law of Resist Not Evil: Our mind kingdom accepts only good and denies evil entry.
6 Law of Unconditional Love: We think - feel only Good God thoughts towards all.
7 Law of Giving and Receiving: What we sow in inner thought, we reap in outer life.
8 Law of Creative Imagination: We mentally picture our desire as already done.
9 Law of Creative Thought: What we think in our heart, we actualize in our life.
10 Law of Speaking God's Word in us with authority - knowing it will bear fruit.
11 Law of Universal Subconscious Mind-Spirit that forms our ideas into reality.

CHAPTER SEVEN

STEP CHOICE 7 FOR SPIRITUAL FREEDOM AND POWER

We humbly chose to ask our Father-Mind Mother-Love God within us, to remove our shortcomings by praying daily in His Presence, and living in the circle of prayer or God-Consciousness, to fulfill His will or love-dream-vision purpose for our lives, so we could experience a happy, joyous, prosperous and free creative love life.

HOW TO LIVE IN THE 12-STEP CIRCLE OF PRAYER AND MAKE YOUR DREAMS COME TRUE

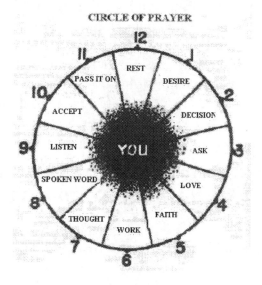

"Delight yourself in the Lord, and He will give you the desires of your heart."
Psalm 37:4

The 12-Steps of the Circle of Prayer that was developed by Stella Terrill Mann and which is illustrated in our diagram is a spiritual growth process that enables us to understand how we receive our God-given love dream ideas through prayer to do God's will and how, with God as our guide, we bring about its fulfillment or manifestation into our outer physical world. These steps apply to all people worldwide and always work when we work them. First let us review how to use our spiritual mental powers of denial and affirmation, and then we will learn the steps of the circle of prayer.

The first step in humbly asking God to remove our shortcomings is to realize that we need to deny the false, negative ideas and beliefs that caused them in the first place, and replace them with new affirmative, positive truth ideas and beliefs. In order to live in the circle of prayer we need to free ourselves from past erroneous beliefs about God, ourselves, and all creation. Denial, as mentioned in previous chapters, is our first step towards wiping out of our minds the mistaken beliefs of a lifetime, and we do this by declaring not to be true a thing that seems true. For instance, if we suffer from low-self-esteem, we have to learn to deny that negative belief and replace it with an affirmative statement of truth that God loves us and created us to have a great self-image of ourselves as His son or daughter. In this way we change our thoughts and beliefs and as a result we change our behaviors and lives. Appearances are directly opposed to all Truth teachings. "Don't judge by appearances, but judge with righteous thinking." Denial brings freedom from bondage to our past ego-self false thoughts and beliefs, and happiness comes when we can effectively deny the power of anything false to touch or trouble us.

The second step is to affirm that all and only good things comes from God. To affirm anything is to assert positively that it is so, even in the face of all contrary evidence, as we did with the above example. God's Infinite Mind is within us and all, and is the substance of every good that we can possibly desire - aye, infinitely more than we are capable of desiring, "for eye has not seen, nor ear heard, nor the human heart conceived, what God has prepared for those who love Him." (Corinthians 2:9) The saying over and over again of any denial or affirmation is a necessary training of our ego-mind that has lived so long in error of false negative beliefs that it needs this constant repetition of Truth affirmations to undress it and to dress it anew. Denials have an erosive or dissolving tendency. Positive affirmations of truth sayings build us up, and give strength and power to our creative thoughts and faith beliefs.

TWELVE UNIVERSAL OR COMMON STEPS OF THE CIRCLE OF PRAYER TO HELP US FULFILL OUR GOD-GIVEN DREAM

1. Desire
2. Decision
3. Ask
4. Love
5. Faith
6. Work
7. Thought
8. Spoken Word
9. Listen
10. Accept
11. Make Disposition
12. Rest

1. Desire: All creation starts with desire.   Desire is the first step in any journey, first movement in any prayer, is a dream-idea in embryo state, a picture of something that could be.   It is a gift from God, a work assignment offered.

2. Decision is free will at work.   Decision is our God-given right to choose.   From this point on, we are on our own unless we ask for help.   Decision opens the floodgates of power for good or evil according to our choice not only about the initial desire, but all through our prayer project.   Indeed, all through our life.

3. Asking in prayer places our order with Master Mind Creative Spirit Power of the Universe.   There are many ways of asking for what we want and need.

4. Love: Love is the law of attraction.   Love is the highest of the spiritual laws.   We will attract, acquire, become that which we love.   We must operate within it if we are to be safe and to build and hold faith.

5. Faith: Faith is the law of correspondences.   Jesus stated the law "believe … receive." Maintaining faith is our greatest problem in life and in working on any dream of our heart's desire.   It is the very "substance of things hoped for." The Holy (Spirit) Servant brings back to us according to our faith.

6. Work: Going into action or work proves our faith and holds it steady.   "Faith without works is dead." And work without faith is deadening to the worker and is largely wasted effort that ends in defeat and frustration.

7. Thought: "As a man thinks in your heart, so is he." The power of creative thought is man's mightiest and in the final analysis includes all his other powers.   It is the least understood, tragically neglected, and misused powers of man.   Wrong thought can bring our circle of good to a grinding halt.

8. Spoken Word: Our word is law.   Our spoken word is the power that we use to tell our Holy Servant what we want it to do for us.   The spoken word means something different from prayer.   It means a Truth statement of fact, a saying it is so.   So Jesus warns us about using idle words, that we shall be both justified and condemned by our own word.   "Every man's word shall be his burden," unless he learns to put wings on them.   Jesus healed the Centurion's servant by speaking the word only.

9. Listen: Listening is a form of accepting and this step must be taken before accepting.   If we believe as we listen we will be certain to act upon that belief sooner or later.   Listening stores the heart.   Reading is a form of listening.   Listening can build or destroy our faith.

10. Accept: Accepting completes the act of giving.   No dream can come true, or prayer can be answered, until the act of accepting takes place.   Accept the best life offers you.   The love of God is the gift and the giver.   Unless we accept we defeat God in His plans for humanity.

11. Distribution: Circulation or passing on what we have received is the law of life.   Right distribution keeps the windows of heaven open.   We must be a good steward.   There's always something we must do when a prayer is answered or a dream comes true.   Here is where tithing of time, love, and money comes in.

12. Rest: To rest is to show active faith in one's self, neighbor, and God. Resting is a time to become free from all hurry, worry, frustration, fear, and tension. It is a time for reflection and evaluating. It is between rest and desire that God impregnates us with new dreams, and inspirational ideas stirring within us.

Now let us review our chart diagram of the circle of prayer and visually see how each of the steps works in unity to help us move from the God-given idea in the kingdom of our mind and heart kingdom to its manifestation in the outer physical world. See clearly that each step is connected with the step opposite it on the chart.

As we review the Circle of prayer diagram and start living in the circle of prayer we begin by affirming that all creation begins with desire, with a dream-idea in embryo, and that our desires are God-given and planted in our conscious mind by God's Universal Subconscious Infinite Mind within our heart. Then through the power of our free will and choice, we decide to accept whether our thought ideas are good or bad ideas. If we ask for God's inner-Spirit guidance, we then know which ideas or desires are God-given and which are not. God's ideas are always for the love and benefit of all people. In going into action with faith, our work is God-guided and so our efforts are not wasted for we are working in line with the circle of prayer and intuitively know that God's in charge and we cannot fail. The substance of the creative thoughts, ideas and words that radiate from within us are being created and formed by God's Subconscious Mind in our outer physical world. This is the meaning of the Scripture quote, "As you think in your heart (subconscious mind), so shall you be." In asking for what we want in our prayers, we must state specifically what we mean and mean what we say. 'Every man's word shall be his burden,' until he learns how to use his words correctly. When we learn to put wings on our words like wings on birds, we find that our spoken words have the power to go forth and return to us whatever we sent them out to accomplish.

The power of your spoken word comes from knowing that you are One with your Father-Mother God, and that when you speak your word of faith, it is in fact a Word of God that you are sending forth as a son or daughter of God as Jesus taught and demonstrated for us. Listening to God's inner-Spirit guidance small voice and inspirational ideas always helps us build our faith, so that we are at-one with God's purpose for us. Being at-one also means that we accept God's will and the comfort of knowing our dreams are God-given, and that they will come true, thus completing the act of God giving us what we ask, and our receiving and passing it on to others.

As God gives to us, so must we pass on what God has done for us to others. This is law of mutual exchange. It is in passing on our God-given gifts and talents that we give back with love what we have so graciously received. This is called the secret of tithing. The successful tither always believes his dream-desires and gifted talents come from God. He talks with God, listens to God and accepts all help offered from God as his Senior Partner, for he believes that all the work he is doing is for the good of all humanity and the glory of God. After sharing what God has done for us we have to learn to rest and reflect in order to restore our spirit, mind and body, and restore our inward reservoirs of strength. It is just as important to rest and play as it is to pray. While we are resting, reflecting and playing, God is preparing us for yet another dream-vision-mission, for He continuously calls us to come up higher because He needs us to fulfill His purposes. Shall we accept it? It only takes one second to receive an idea, desire, or thought from God directly that can change your life forever. As you pray and receive God's intention or will or dream desire you can be sure that it will bless you and all humanity, and glorify our Father-Mother God.

LOVE LESSONS TO REMEMBER

Learn to deny your erroneous ego-self thinking thoughts from entering your mind.

Learn to affirm only good God Truth thoughts to enter your subconscious mind.

All prayers start with a God-given desire to change our thoughts and situations.

You have the God-given power to decide to accept or reject any and all thoughts.

Ask God to guide you to live in the circle of prayer in fulfilling your dream-desires.

Go into action and work in faith with God towards achieving your prayer goals.

Inspirational God thoughts and ideas will radiate through you and your work.

Listening to the thoughts of God within you will give you purpose for your life.

Accept your God-given love dream-desires and vision purpose for your life.

Share what God has done for you and pass it on to others to glorify God.

Rest and play, so you can be ready for your next God-given prayer vision-mission.

Become aware that God needs to work in you and as you to fulfill His plans, and He is glorified when you trust in Him to fulfill your love dream-vision-mission for good.

MEDITATION

The circle of prayer is the way we live, and work in, and with, God's Spirit-Mind-Love-Life within us, to fulfill His will and our God-given love-dream-vision-mission for our lives by individualizing and expressing His purpose for us for all humanity. Through prayer, God, the Universal Subconscious Master Mind or Love Spirit, impregnates our conscious mind with inspirational thoughts and dream ideas, through the power of our creative imagination, at the center of our consciousness. I now focus and rest in God and listen to His still small voice in my heart and mind kingdom calling me to be about His business, and I am open and receptive to His dream vision-mission ideas for me.

RECOMMENDED READINGS

How to Live in the Circle of Prayer and Make Your dreams Come True, by Stella Terrill Mann, Published by Unity Books, 1959.

Three Magic Words, by U.S. Andersen, Published by Wilshire Book Company, 1954

Lessons in Truth, by H. Emilie Cady, Published by Unity School of Christianity, 1946

CHAPTER EIGHT

STEP CHOICE 8 FOR SPIRITUAL FREEDOM AND POWER

We chose to accept God's love and forgiveness for our mistakes, and became willing to make amends to all who had harmed us to be at peace with all people, and focus on fulfilling God's will and love-dream purpose for us for the good of all humanity.

THE AMAZING LAW OF FORGIVENESS & PEACE OF MIND

"Forgive us our trespasses as we forgive those who trespass against us."

We all desire peace of mind and soul, and God has provided us with the spiritual mental law and power to achieve this state of consciousness in our heart and mind kingdom. We have the power to ask God to forgive us all our mistakes and shortcomings, and having received God's love and forgiveness, we must do the same and forgive those who harm us by praying for them, and setting ourselves free from all the mental poisons of anger, ill-will, and resentment thoughts and feelings.

Forgiveness does not mean we condone or approve of other people's error ways and the harm they have caused us, but we see clearly now in God-Consciousness that we cannot afford to be separated from them, because we now know that we all live in One Universal God Mind-Spirit, whose law of life is love and peace and unity, and not war and separation which is egotism. Now that we dwell in God-Consciousness we become aware that whenever we are angry and resentful toward others we in fact give our power of mental peace over to others without knowing we have done so. Whenever we allow anger or resentments to rule our heart and mind kingdom we have let others take us prisoners in our own mind because we are negatively attached to anyone we allow to upset us. That is why Jesus, our Master-Teacher of spiritual mental law taught us to forgive others and bless them instead. He understood the mental and emotional law and power of negative thinking mental poisons, and gave us the spiritual solution of how to control our mind thoughts and heart feelings, through the law of forgiveness and peace of mind.

Now we come to understand that our real enemies are within ourselves, within our own mind kingdom, within our inner thoughts and feelings. The Bible says, 'A man's enemies shall be of his own household,' which means of his own mind and heart. We are now learning in this step choice that we need to learn how to control our mind and heart kingdom through daily prayer and meditation in God's Spirit-Mind-Love Presence. As we do this, we will learn how to control what thoughts and feelings we allow to enter our mind and heart kingdom by disciplining our mind.

By allowing and affirming only good God-thoughts to enter our mind, and denying entry to negative and destructive thoughts and feelings, we start to understand the spiritual mental law of mind, which is, that whatever seed thoughts we sow in our heart and mind kingdom we always reap a similar harvest. If we think good, good follows, if we think evil, evil follows.

As we learn to pray and make direct conscious contact with God's Universal Subconscious Infinite Mind and Love Spirit within us, we learn we have received the spiritual mental power to choose what thoughts we let in to our heart and mind kingdom, which Jesus called our 'Secret Place,' where we meet personally with our Father-Mother God. Here we unite our mind with God's Master Mind Spirit, and His Infinite power works through us to rule our mind with love. This is why we need to choose to make amends to others. This is God's way of teaching us to be His sons and daughters and to be peacemakers, instead of warmongers. This is how much our God loves us, and created us in His image and likeness to individualize as us.

Now we come to the Serenity Prayer in which we pray to God to teach us to know what we can change and what we cannot change and the wisdom to know the difference. It is a universal prayer used each day and needs to be understood by all.

OUR WILLINGNESS TO PASS ON GOD'S FORGIVENESS TO ALL

The Serenity Prayer: "God grant us the serenity to accept the things we cannot change, the courage to change the things we can, and the wisdom to know the difference."

The key to this Serenity Prayer is becoming aware of the spiritual understanding which has come into our consciousness from the peace and forgiveness of God. Without this spiritual understanding that God has forgiven us all our mistakes, we would not have the humility and love to do the same for others. We grow by using for others the light and knowledge we have received from God. When it is time and we choose to be at peace with all, God places the desire in our heart to be willing to make amends to all persons we have harmed, and the courage to do so to achieve the peace of mind and freedom that God intends for us to experience.

We become aware that we have the God-given power to choose to accept others just as they are without condemnation just as God has accepted us. We realize by God's grace that we cannot change others and that peace comes from accepting them just as they are. For now we see with God's eyes that they too are loved and need to be accepted by us just as God accepted us when we came to Him broken-hearted and full of guilt, shame and fear seeking His forgiveness and peace.

This God consciousness eliminates our false ego consciousness of separation that always looked to be better than others because of our inferiority or superiority attitudes. As we go forth we realize that the only power we have is to let God change our inner thinking attitudes and beliefs. We now understand clearly that we have the God-given power and courage to change our own thoughts and feelings about all the people we meet in all our relationships. This is what we have the power to change - ourselves with God's help working in us. It is always an 'inside job.'

Thanks be to God for this spiritual understanding for it is the beginning and the end of our isolation from God, ourselves, and all other people. This truth has set us free, and we are now at peace and in harmony with God, ourselves and other people. Thus we willingly accept others just as they are and we make amends with love and acceptance without leaving a void for old resentments to crawl back in at a later date. The truth has set us free from our false egotistic-self thinking thoughts of separation from others, which is the very worst addiction or sin in the world.

This truth, peace and love reconciliation with all God's sons and daughters, gives us the power and vision to see clearly the way to change our personality, to let go of our small, false ego-self and put on our new identity as inner-Spirit-guided sons and daughters of God. This new God-Consciousness of spiritual-self and faith in God gives us the courage to seek God's will for us and do the work God calls us to do. Now, filled with God's love and peace and vision for our lives, we are ready to individualize His Spirit-Mind-Love-Life within us. We are now aware that we all dwell in God's One Divine Mind or Spirit Presence, and we have the courage and willingness to go forth to fulfill our God-given dreams for the good and love of all.

Now, with spiritual understanding of what making amends means, we go forth to make direct amends that will liberate us from our past ego-separation from God, ourselves and all people, and that will free us to be about our Father-Mother God's business… the vision to see, the faith to believe, and the courage to do God's will.

LOVE LESSONS TO REMEMBER

We learn that we need to forgive and accept others, just as God forgives and accepts us in spite of all our past mistakes, to be at peace.

We let go of our false ego-self ideas of inferiority or superiority or separation in all our relationships, and we let love and acceptance into our heart and mind kingdom.

We are willing to let God work through us to change our false ego-self separation consciousness and become One as inner-Spirit-directed sons and daughters of God.

Daily we pray the Serenity Prayer: God grant me the Serenity to accept the things I cannot change – other people, the courage to change the things I can – my own thoughts and feelings and attitudes, and the wisdom to know the difference. Thus, we experience love and peace and unity of the Spirit in all our relationships.

We give thanks to God daily by saying the Serenity Prayer to make us aware we can only change ourselves, our thoughts and feelings, and we cannot change others, and this God-Truth sets us free from giving our power away and brings peace with all.

Our willingness to make amends is God's Spirit-Mind courage working in us to do the things we could not do of ourselves, and we know God is love and works in all people for unity and peace in the fellowship of the Spirit.

MEDITATION

The willingness of God to forgive us and bring peace in our lives gives us the vision to see ourselves as we truly are, and the faith to be willing to make amends to all people with this new God-Consciousness within us. Our willingness to be at peace with all people is an affirmative action that sets into motion our God-given power to love and understand and choose the spoken words we will speak to others and the feelings we will portray when we go and make our amends to all the people we have harmed including ourselves. Seek to be willing to let God's Spirit-Mind guide you as you go forth to make your amends, for it is God's desire for you to be always loving and forgiving toward all people in your life so you can experience love and peace and unity in your heart and mind kingdom.

Each day as I awake in our Father-Mother God's Spirit-Mind-Love-Life Presence, Peace and Power I send out my love to all people and forgive all who have harmed me in any way as God's love has forgiven me, so I can experience the freedom of being at-one with all my brothers and sisters worldwide. I say the Serenity Prayer – God, grant me the serenity to accept the things I cannot change - other people – the courage to change the things I can – my own thoughts and feelings – and the wisdom to know the difference. Thank you Father-Mother God for teaching me and guiding me in Thy thoughts, words and deeds today, and may I do thy will and love always!

RECOMMENDED READINGS

The Sermon on the Mount, by Emmet Fox, Published by Harper & Row, 1934.

Alcoholics Anonymous, Published by Alcoholics Anonymous, Inc., 1939.

How To Live in the Circle of Prayer and Make Your Dreams Come True, by Stella Terrill Mann, Published by Unity Books, 1954.

CHAPTER NINE

STEP CHOICE 9: VISION TO SEE – FAITH TO BELIEVE – COURAGE TO DO

We chose to trust God's Inner-Spirit guidance and were given the courage to make amends to all people we had harmed to heal all our relationships and be at peace with all.   As we did so we let go of our ego- separation from others and entered into the unity and fellowship of God's One Universal Subconscious Master-Mind-Love-Spirit as sons or daughters.

YOU HAVE THE GOD-GIVEN POWER TO CONTROL WHAT THOUGHTS ENTER INTO YOUR HEART & MIND KINGDOM

> *"As you sow (thought seeds you accept and allow to enter your heart*
> *or subconscious mind), so shall you reap."*
> *Galatians 6:7*

The law of being at one with God's inner-Spirit-Mind guidance allows us to control the thoughts our conscious mind accepts and allows to enter our heart kingdom or subconscious mind.   As we learn how to use God's spiritual laws of mind, love, and life within us, we find the courage to go forth and make amends with all people and are set free from bondage to the mental poisons of fear, anger, and resentment.   By using our God-given power of choosing which thoughts and feelings we allow to enter our heart and mind kingdom all our relationships are healed by our new found God-given freedom of thought control for peace of mind at all times.

VISION TO SEE – FAITH TO BELIEVE – COURAGE TO DO

"Without a vision the people perish.   With a vision the people flourish."

VISION TO SEE: God, the Universal Subconscious Master-Mind-Love-Spirit is our dream-giver and calls us to manifest the dream ideas and desires or vision He places in our heart and mind kingdom as a love and life mission for us to accomplish.   This is why we can truthfully say from our own personal experience that God's will for us is always our heart's desire.   Our dream-vision-mission is exactly tailor-made for our own unique individual gifts and talents.   It is exactly what we would have loved to personally be and do with our lives in order to contribute to the well-being of all humanity, and which at one time in our life journey, we thought was just a far-fetched wish that would never materialize.   Now our Father-Mother God awakens us to its reality, and now we know we have God as our Senior Partner to provide us with all we need to fulfill His God-given love dream-vision-mission.   We cannot fail for one with God is a majority.   Ask God to reveal His will and purpose for your life, and the answer will be revealed.

Our revelation, vision, and mission to establish God's Spiritual Freedom Centre for New Thought Spirituality, Science of Mind and addictions-recovery worldwide was given in August of 2001.   It was a God-given dream to set His people free from bondage to all types of false man-made religious beliefs, or mental addictions or poisons that were separating them from their true spiritual identity and powers as sons and daughters of God.   The general dream-vision-mission was given but much work had to be done to bring it to the physical manifestation it has achieved today, and the program work will continue to improve and get better with God's ever loving guidance for the freedom of all His people.

FAITH TO BELIEVE: We now understand that whatever our conscious mind can conceive of, or creatively visualize, or imagine, or picture in our mind's eye is the substance that God, the Universal Subconscious Mind or Spirit creates into our physical world.   First the God-given dream idea, thought and desire in our mind's eye coupled with our faith conviction feeling that God can create this desired good into our lives, and then, the manifestation.   This is what is meant by the Bible words "Faith is the substance of things hoped for, the evidence of things not seen." First, conceive in the invisible God-given Spirit-Mind world of ideas and desire and faith, then manifest the dream into the visible physical world.   Thus we see that God has given us the power and three step formula, that I received from Norman Vincent Peale a few years ago, to creatively prayerize, visualize, and actualize our dream desires by our thoughts and creative imagination; and as you believe faithfully that "with God all things are possible, it will be done unto you according to your faith."

Now we are learning how to use the law of supply and demand, which is to 'ask and you receive.' Knowing that it is God who provides the inspirational thoughts, ideas, or desires within our heart and mind, and not just our small separate ego-self, is absolutely essential for us to understand.   God is the Source and Substance of all our ideas for 'we live and move and have our being in One Divine Mind or Spirit at all times.' It is only a false belief or error thinking to think we are ever separated from God who dwells in the heart, or subconscious mind of us all to fulfill His purposes.

COURAGE TO DO: God has a plan for every person and we can each discover the purpose through prayer and meditation in our heart and mind kingdom, which Jesus called our Secret Place. It is where we talk with our Father-Mother God and listen for the answers to our questions or just chat in His Loving Presence, Peace and Power.   Now that we know that God wills and works through us to achieve His purposes, we realize that this is true of all people who surrender their false ego-self to God's Spirit-Mind will, and seek to be peacemakers and equal-souled with all.

If you are now ready to let go of your false ego-self, and follow your God-given inner Spirit guidance and love dream-vision-mission you need to pray and meditate daily in His Presence to receive your daily bread or inspirational God-given ideas to live a happy, joyous, prosperous and free life individualizing and expressing God within you.   Here are some daily meditations or creative mental and emotional ideas to help you move up the ladder of accomplishing your God-given love dream-vision mission which I received through and pass on to you from my friends Don and Bernice Curtis as an answer to prayer.

12 CREATIVE IDEAS & ATTITUDES ON THE LADDER OF ACCOMPLISHMENT

(in Chapter 3 of Don and Bernice Curtis' book
"Your Thoughts Can Change Your Life")

Align yourself with these 12 creative mental and emotional ideas.   Get quiet inside and let your mind dwell on them.   Speak in simple direct statements with a feeling of conviction that what you are saying is really true.   God, the Universal Subconscious Master-Mind-Love-Spirit accepts the suggestions you give It by your conscious mind, and works to create and manifest your desires in your outer life conditions.

1. THE CREATIVE MENTAL-EMOTIONAL LAW & POWER ATTITUDE OF RELAXATION

I now quietly release myself from all outer concern.   I let my mind go free as I relax completely.   I am relaxed physically, mentally and emotionally.   I am free from all pressures and tensions.   I am attuned to the free, full flow of Life moving through me.   I let go and let God take over.   I am now co-operating with God's free Creative Spirit-Mind-Love.   All resistance is dissolved and I am ready for creative action.

2. THE CREATIVE MENTAL-EMOTIONAL LAW & POWER ATTITUDE OF EXPECTATION

I expect the best of life today. I expect to do my best and expect the best from other people. I expect the harmonious and beneficial working out of every situation. I expect to give happiness. I expect good health in my mind, my body and my world of affairs. I expect an abundance of all things. I have more than enough to meet all my requirements. I thrill to the expectancy of living life abundantly today.

3. THE CREATIVE MENTAL-EMOTIONAL LAW & POWER ATTITUDE OF RECOGNITION

There is One Life, One Infinite Intelligence and Boundless Love Source - God - at the center of all people, places and things. Today I recognize God's Loving Presence, Peace and Power flowing through all creation. I feel His Presence in every part of my being. I am aware of law and order back of all manifestation. I enjoy the prolific spontaneous beauty in all of nature. I know there is only One Cause back of every effect. I recognize the privilege and potential of being a son or daughter of God. I know there is more to know and so I let my mind expand into infinity today.

4. THE CREATIVE MENTAL-EMOTIONAL LAW & POWER ATTITUDE OF UNIFICATION

Whatever life is, I am living it. Whatever God is, I am expressing It. Whatever truth is, I embody it. I am an individualized expression of God, the great mystery of life. I am one with all life. I am one with all people. I am unified with God, the Great Cause which is the Creator of all living things. I am a brother or sister to every living thing. I embody the Spirit spark of divinity. My mind is my use of the One Divine Mind or Spirit of God. My soul is one with the Soul of the Universe. I can never be alone. All separation is dissolved as I attune myself to the oneness of God's life in me and all creation today.

5. THE CREATIVE MENTAL-EMOTIONAL LAW & POWER ATTITUDE OF DEDICATION

I am happy to be alive today. I know who I am, where I am going, and what I am here to do. I dedicate my life to the expression of good. I discover what I can do better than anyone else, and I dedicate my being, talent, ability and efforts to the service of God-Humanity. I am dedicated to living life fully today. I determine to do the best I can at all times and in every situation.   I find my right place in life and I co-operate with the forces of love, growth and expansion.   I love life and love to live.   I love people and I dedicate myself to love and helping make the world a better place for all humanity.   Happy, purposeful, and abundant loving and living is my dedication now.   Thanks be to God.

6. THE CREATIVE MENTAL-EMOTIONAL LAW & POWER ATTITUDE OF INTENTION

I intend to succeed at anything and everything I undertake.   I choose my objectives wisely and I intend to follow them through.   I am filled with good God intentions, and I do something about them.   I intend to be a better person, and I start right now.   I intend to express love and goodwill for all people, and I start right now.   I intend to be happy, joyous, prosperous and free, so no other thought ever enters my mind.   I intend to succeed at being creative love in action, and so naturally I am successful.   I have every intention of making this day the best day I've ever lived.   I intend to make my contribution to life today, and I start with this creative God-given love dream-vision-mission.

7. THE CREATIVE MENTAL-EMOTIONAL LAW & POWER ATTITUDE OF IDENTIFICATION

I am one with the object of my desire.   I live my God-given dreams completely.   I think, feel, breathe, taste, eat, drink and sleep my goals and objectives.   I have a singleness of purpose. My life has focus and meaning as I provide a vital point into which God's Creative Mind-Spirit energy of life can flow.   There is no place where God leaves off and I begin.   I identify myself with the All-Good who is God, so I become one with that good.   I look like the creative ideas in my mind.   I act like someone who is identified with loving purpose, service and good deeds. This is the truth.   I am grateful for God's call.

8. THE CREATIVE MENTAL-EMOTIONAL LAW & POWER ATTITUDE OF CONVICTION

There is no doubt in my mind today.   I am convinced that I can go where I want to go, do what I want to do, and be what I want to be.   This is my conviction, so it is true for me.   My thoughts and feelings blend together in forming my conviction.   My conviction indicates the level of my faith.   I carry the conviction of success.   My subconscious mind is working for good because of my constant conviction of good.   I know all things are working out for the best.   I know that right action is taking place in my plans and projects.   I know I am growing, and I know I am achieving.   I do my best at all times to give to life the abundant loving good which I am convinced life gives to me.   God - Love does such things!

9. THE CREATIVE MENTAL-EMOTIONAL LAW & POWER ATTITUDE OF REALIZATION

Right here and now I realize the truth of these statements of good. I have convinced my subconscious mind that I am a spiritual being, just as the inspiration of God, the Universal Subconscious Master-Mind-Love-Spirit gave the realization to my mind. I am free! I am whole! I am bright, and clean and new. I have a fresh realization of the meaning of life. It's not what I get, it's what I give. It's not what people think of me, but what I feel for them! Today I realize that I live forever, and that this moment is the most important time of my life. All of my dreams have come true. I realize many things. I revel in the realization of my fondest expectations. I gratefully realize the goodness of God at all times.

10. THE CREATIVE MENTAL-EMOTIONAL LAW & POWER ATTITUDE OF PROJECTION

I let my realization and visualization of good go before me and prepare the way. My dreams precede me. What I am is visible from afar. My every thought, feeling and deed is a messenger and a servant. I proclaim the good news from the housetops. I exude confidence, authority, strength and love. I know what I can do and people know that I can and will do it. My consciousness reaches to untold heights. My ideas, thoughts, and undertakings are the Spirit-led, God-Mind-guided channels through which my loving goodness is shared with the world. I hold nothing back. I share all that I have, and my God-Consciousness reaches the stars. I am projected into total life today by the power of knowing.

11. THE CREATIVE MENTAL-EMOTIONAL LAW & POWER ATTITUDE OF ACTION

I must be about my Father-Mother God's business. Today I get out and get going. I stir the stagnant waters and give them fresh release. I go to work and accomplish mighty deeds. I go where I need to go and do what I need to do. I flex my muscles and put them to work. I tackle the thing that cannot be done and I do it. I do not know what boredom and inactivity are. I am a doer. First I pray for guidance and strength, then I act knowing that God, the Universal Subconscious Master-Mind-Love-Spirit, is working in me and all people and circumstances. I join thought, feeling and action into a mighty team of accomplishment. I won't sit around and wait. I work in harmony with the creative law of love, belief and life today. Together we get things done. I am set to go. I act intelligently now.

12. THE CREATIVE MENTAL-EMOTIONAL LAW & POWER ATTITUDE OF CO-OPERATION

I know that I can accomplish anything only when I am working in co-operation with God. I am an individualized expression of my Father-Mind Mother-Love God, whose Creative Spirit-Mind dwells in me and all. I co-operate and follow God's inner Spirit guidance and love dream purpose for my life. I do all I can to attune my thoughts, feelings and actions to being about God's will and purpose for me. I flow with life. I feel its free, creative love flowing through me now. I will never resist it. I revel in the release of spiritual mind power through my whole being. I let myself be used by a Power greater than myself. I am on God's team, and I know the meaning of teamwork now. And so it is done dear God!

BREAKING OUT OF THE BOX OF SPACE, TIME & LIMITATION

"You are gods, sons and daughters of the Most High." Jesus Christ

Now you are ready to be inner-Spirit guided by God and claim your God-given powers as a son or daughter of God. You can be anything you desire to be, and do whatever your heart desires, and it will be for your good and the love of all, for you now know who you really are and that your Father-Mother God has set your creative Spirit free to fulfill your God-given dreams. There are no limits to what God can do through you and you now know that with God in you all things are possible to you and that this truth is true for everyone who turns to God within their subconscious mind and makes the decision to be about our Father-Mother God's business. This is the Resurrection Experience we must all claim as Jesus taught and demonstrated for us as our Way-Shower when he said, "I am the way, the truth and the life, you who believe in me as a son or daughter of God shall do the works I do, and greater works, for the Spirit-Mind-Love-Life of God is individualized in you too." Go forth and individualize and express the love of God in you and glorify our Father Mind Mother Love in us all.

LOVE LESSONS TO REMEMBER

As we willingly choose to make amends with all the people we have harmed in the past, God gives us the courage to heal all our relationships and be at peace with all.

We have the God-given power to control our mind, and to choose the true or false seed thoughts we accept to enter our subconscious mind as faith convictions.

Your inner thoughts are creative things that become manifested in your outer physical world by the power of God's Subconscious Mind working in all creation.

God is our dream-giver and has a tailor-made purpose or love dream-vision-mission for each and every person when we seek God's will for us with all our heart.

Through meditation you can focus your mind's eye attention on creative mental and emotional attitudes and powers like intention, dedication, unification, action, etc.

You have the God-given power to break out of the box of ego-world beliefs that you were programmed to believe in by outer authorities when you were young and impressionable. By being inner-Spirit guided you become God-Conscious and free.

We are all created in the image and likeness of God as sons and daughters with all the spiritual mental faculties and powers of our Father-Mother God. As we claim our inheritance and identity we're set free of ego-self imposed fears and limitations.

Learn to understand and know how to use your God-given spiritual mental powers, and laws of mind as a son or daughter of God-Consciousness to fulfill your destiny.

MEDITATION

When I pass the place of ego-arrogance and doubt, and enter into the fullness of God-Consciousness, I am inner Spirit guided in my ways of communicating with others in a loving and caring way. With new found courage, purpose and conviction I am able to make amends to all people I have harmed in the past and heal all my past relationships, and start fresh new peaceful relationships with all by trusting God to work in and through me. The admittance of my past mistakes to those I have harmed, and making of amends to them releases my consciousness into a new level of freedom from bondage to ego-arrogance, doubts and actions I once acted out in my life. Now I know that I am not alone in making my decisions just by myself, but I am united with the infinite intelligence, wisdom and love of God. This releases and sets me free from the false ego-self baggage of false beliefs that I carried in my mind and actions and reactions towards other people in my past. I now replace these false, negative thoughts immediately with positive good God thoughts and beliefs in my subconscious mind so that I don't leave a void or deep dark hole where negative thoughts can creep back into my heart and mind. Now I focus and let only good God thoughts do the work, and I speak words of love, truth, and peace that unite me with other people and let go of all negative, reactive ego-self-thoughts of separation, because I know that "With God all things are possible including making amends."

RECOMMENDED READINGS

Your Thoughts Can Change Your Life, by Donald Curtis, Published by Prentice Hall, Inc. 1961

The Power of Positive Thinking, by Norman Vincent Peale, Published by Prentice Hall, Inc. 1952.

Power Through Constructive Thinking, by Emmet Fox, Published by Harper & Row, 1932.

The Magic In Your Mind, by U.S. Andersen, Published by Wilshire Book Company, 1961.

STAGE 4 CHOICES

THE TRANSFORMING EXPERIENCE INTO GOD-CONSCIOUSNESS AND PASSING ON THE GOOD NEWS TO OTHERS

 **SPIRITUAL FREEDOM CENTRE – A 4-Stage Program for New Thought Spirituality & Addictions-Recovery**

STAGE 4 STEPS FOR SPIRITUAL SELF–DISCOVERY-RECOVERY CHOICES OR CHANGES OF CONSCIOUSNESS FOR A NEW LIFE

<u>Stage 4 Steps 10-11-12: Becoming Aware of God's Will & Purpose for Us.</u>
<u>We Daily Apply the Spiritual-Mental Laws of Mind, Love & Life.</u>

10)   We choose to take personal inventory, and when we were wrong promptly admitted it to maintain our peace of mind and serenity.

-    We choose to stay aware of our God-given daily guidance.

-    We choose to be at peace with our thoughts and all relationships.

11)   We choose to seek through prayer and meditation to improve our conscious contact with God as we understand Him, praying, only for knowledge of His will for us, and the power to carry that out.

-    We choose to pray daily to do God's will: to love and serve all.

-    We choose every morning and evening to thank God for His help.

12)   Having had a spiritual awakening as a result of these steps, we choose to carry this message to other egotists, and practice these spiritual principles in all our affairs.

-    We choose to freely receive God's love and pass it on to others.

-    Healed by God's Love, we choose to become the wounded healers.

SPIRITUAL FREEDOM CENTRE – A 4-Stage Program for New Thought Spirituality & Addictions-Recovery

STAGE 4 CHOICES TO DEVELOP OUR SPIRITUAL CHARACTER TRAITS & USE OUR LAWS OF MIND TO FULFILL OUR DREAMS

Stage 4 Choices: The Transformative Love-Vision-Mission Experience: We Pass On God's Blessings as the Light of the World and Salt of the Earth."

1   Law of God-given Talents of Love, Faith, Thinking, Imagination, Prayer, and Praise.
2   Law of Speaking our Word of Power to free and heal the wounded and lost.
3   Law of Faith or Belief to manifest our God-given dreams of love and service.
4   Law of Sharing our Stories of God's blessings to give others love, faith, and hope.
5   Law of Prayer-Mediation in God's Presence and Power to rise above all problems.
6   Law of Living a God–centered, inner Spirit-guided life, and teach love by example.
7   Law of claiming our Spiritual Identity - that with God in us all things are possible!
8   Law of Mind: "As you think in your heart - your subconscious mind, so are you."
9   Law of Identification as a son or daughter of God-Consciousness and powers.
10 Law of accepting God as Source of all ideas, dreams, peace, joy, supply, and freedom.
11 Law of transforming our scars into healing balm to heal our wounded friends.
12 Law of Redemption: Through God's grace we became wounded healers for all.
13 Law of Attraction: We pray daily giving thanks, and ask for creative thoughts to love and serve all in the freedom and fellowship of God's Spirit and will for us.
14 Law of becoming a Light of the world, salt of the earth & glorify God's Name.

CHAPTER TEN

STEP CHOICE 10: WE HAVE THE POWER TO CHOOSE OUR OWN HEAVEN OR HELL

We chose to take a daily personal inventory of ourselves by seeking God's inner-Spirit guidance and power to control our heart and mind kingdom by sowing only good God thought seeds and promptly deny entry to any negative mental poison thoughts into the garden of our heart-mind, in order to maintain our new thought spirituality, identity, unity, and fellowship as sons and daughters of God.

GOD HAS GIVEN US ALL THE POWER OF CHOICE TO CREATE OUR OWN HEAVEN OR HELL!

Every day of our lives we choose our own heaven or hell depending on the thoughts, feelings, ideas and beliefs we choose to focus on. Many of us at one time were completely ignorant, or unaware, of how to use our God-given power of choice. We each have the equal power of choice, to choose which thoughts and feelings we will dwell upon and entertain on any given day. Many of us are completely unaware or ignorant of the fact that we live in a God-given mental universe, and that our inner mind thoughts are causative, creative and formative; that whatever we choose to think and feel and believe in within our heart and mind kingdom is always eventually expressed in our outer life conditions, circumstances and relationships.

The spiritual mental law is that whatever you think and believe in grows. So what is the solution? How can you change your thinking, your thoughts, feelings and beliefs so that you only experience good and harmony and peace in your life? Scientific prayer is the answer. As you turn inward and meet with God in the Secret Place of your heart and mind consciousness and learn to observe the thoughts coming at you, you receive the guidance, inspiration, enlightenment, and empowerment to control the thoughts, feelings, and beliefs you allow to enter your mind or house. As you learn and practice this mental diet exercise, you control your thoughts and life.

Now do you understand more clearly what we mean when we say that we choose our own heaven (harmony and peace and love thoughts), or choose our own hell, (negative, mental poison thoughts like anger, resentment, ill-will to enter our garden kingdom. Another Bible quote that is relevant here is, "as you think in your heart, - or subconscious mind, - so shall you be." Both are universal psychological and scientific truths that apply to everyone no matter what their creed, color, sex or race beliefs may be. We all have the God-given power to choose to build a heaven or hell for ourselves. No one can take this freedom from us unless we allow it and let other outer authorities to make our choices for us. All of us have done this at one time or another in our lives, but at that time, we were unaware or ignorant of what we were doing. So now let us always take the time each day through a personal mental inventory to choose what thoughts, feelings and beliefs we will accept or deny entry into our heart and mind kingdom, the Secret Place of God within our subconscious.

A DAILY PERSONAL INVENTORY HELPS MAINTAIN OUR NEW THOUGHT SPIRITUALITY & GOD-CONSCIOUSNESS

Each of us is responsible for the thoughts, feelings and beliefs we accept into our mind and heart kingdom, and we can control this by making a daily personal inventory of our mental diet for the day. The choice of truly looking within ourselves with love and honesty will correct our ways of thinking, and then our actions will radiate outward towards all other persons according to our thoughts.

"As within so without," is a universal law of mind and life for as you think in your subconscious mind, or heart, so shall you act and behave. Our mental inner thoughts and beliefs are always manifested in our actions as effects. If in doing a daily personal inventory, we run into erroneous negative thinking on our part during the day, we have the God-given power to choose to promptly change our thinking to positive thoughts and to make amends quickly before any further damage is done in our relationships with others. This is the meaning of the Bible saying, "A man's enemies shall be of his own household," in his own mind.

A daily personal inventory helps us observe our thoughts and make correct choices and decisions to build upon as we choose, to have our thoughts be in tune with good God thoughts at all times. Each step choice you make is an 'inside job' leading you out of the outer ego self-centered world of separation from others, into a spiritual conscious plane that unites you with everyone, and changes you from within into God's image and likeness as a son or daughter of God. This God-Consciousness comes about by trusting God's inner spirit guidance within you, and gives you the courage to do your personal mental inventory for the betterment of yourself and all people. It is in this state of God-Consciousness that you seek to think and do only what is best for yourself and all others. You learn 'to be true to your own self, and then you can never be false to anyone,' as Shakespeare so wisely found out and shared with us. By being honest, truthful, and loving in your thoughts, words and actions with other people, without fear of other people's opinions, you learn to detach from the situation and listen and follow only your own inner Spirit guidance. This God given power to rightly choose to affirm only good thoughts and deny negative thoughts, feelings and beliefs from entering your mind and heart kingdom is the explanation to the cure for living in harmony, love and peace with our Father-Mind Mother-Love God, and all people worldwide. This is what it means to be an inner-Spirit-led, or a God-guided and directed spiritual human being.

In doing these step choices and learning to practice living daily in these life choices of love, harmony and understanding, we start to pass on what we have received and radiate that God-Consciousness out from us to all other people. It is through our own example of living, feeling, sharing, and praying that we are able to receive new inspirational God-ideas, and go into deeper depths of understanding by expressing our new found identity as sons and daughters of God-Consciousness.

LOVE LESSONS TO REMEMBER

"A man's enemies shall be of his own house," (mind thoughts and feelings)

"Gather treasure in heaven:" fill your heart and mind with good God thoughts.

"As within, so without," is the universal law of mind because we live in a mental universe, and 'as we think in our heart (subconscious mind), so are we.'

"The kingdom of God is within you," means that God's Holy Spirit-Mind-Love- Life dwells within you, and is guiding you to choose and control the thoughts you let into your mind and heart kingdom whether good or bad.

"Whatever you think about grows!" The thought seeds you sow in your inner mind kingdom and believe in grow and reap a harvest, or manifest in your outer physical world conditions and environment.

We thank God for His inner Mind or Spirit Presence and Power within us, in guiding, inspiring, enlightening, and empowering us through daily direct conscious prayer contact to choose only good God thoughts and denying entry to negative ego-destructive mental poisons from entering our mind kingdom.

We now know with certainty that "we all live and move and have our being" in God's One Universal Everywhere Present Subconscious Mind and Boundless Love-Spirit within us all.

We each and all must do our own work in taking the spiritual step choices that lead to spiritual freedom and claim and use our God-given spiritual mental powers to have dominion over our lives or mind kingdom ... for truly God's Mind or Spirit is in us as sons and daughters of God.

"Let this mind be in you that was also in Christ Jesus who thought it not robbery to be equal with God." Like Jesus we must claim our God powers.

A daily personal inventory means seeking daily guidance and union with God in controlling our mind and heart kingdom so that we think and act in tune with God's Consciousness and will for us for the good of all.

What kind of mental thought company are you keeping in your heart on a daily basis? Is it thoughts that unite you with all or negative thoughts that separate you from all?

MEDITATION

(in U.S. Andersen's book "Three Magic Words"

Today I thank God that His Presence, Peace, Power and Divine Mind directs my daily thinking, feelings, actions, and for knowing that we all live, and move, and have our being in His One Universal Subconscious Mind-Spirit within us all.   There is a Power within me which I can use to overcome all obstacles, solve all problems, a Power that flows from the farthest reaches of the universe, out of the infinite, omnipotent Master Mind-Spirit of God.   I give over my work, its progress and path, to Him.   No matter the negative thoughts I encounter today, I see beyond them, and I perceive their other face.   I know God is all things at all times; therefore I affirm the positive.   My new found God-Consciousness surpasses the limitations, fears, and sense of separation of my false ego-self, and soars out to encompass all beings, and all life in the Spirit-Mind Love of God.   By knowing the divine and loving the Divine I am assured that His Power will work in and through me to illustrate to the world the divinity of man.   By the grace of God I now have a new identity as a son or daughter of God which is the Truth about all people everywhere at all times.   Today with God's help I can choose to have only good God thoughts and love feelings towards all people.   I am at peace, and in harmony with all creation, and I give God thanks for all my blessings, and the awareness that we all individualize and express the One Divine Spirit-Mind-Love-Life of God within us all as sons and daughters.

RECOMMENDED READINGS

The Sermon on the Mount, by Emmet Fox, Published by Harper & Row, 1934.

Alcoholics Anonymous, Published by Alcoholics Anonymous, Inc., 1939.

The Magic in Your Mind, by U.S Andersen, Published by Wilshire Book Company, 1961.

The Power of Your Subconscious Mind, by Joseph Murphy, Published by Prentice Hall, Inc, 1963.

CHAPTER ELEVEN

STEP CHOICE 11 - PRAYER IS THE WAY TO FIND AND FULFILL OUR GOD-GIVEN IDENTITY, POWERS & DREAMS

We chose by daily prayer and meditation to make direct conscious contact with God's Infinite Mind and Boundless Love within our subconscious mind, praying only for the knowledge of our Father-Mother God's will, or love dream purpose to fulfill our lives, and the power to carry that out, by claiming our God-given spiritual mental powers and identity as sons and daughters of God.

PRAYER POWER UNITES US DIRECTLY WITH OUR FATHER-MOTHER GOD WHO ANSWERS ALL OUR PRAYER REQUESTS!

"Seek ye first the kingdom of God (the Spirit-Mind-Love Consciousness of God in you, and His love dream purpose to fulfill your life) and all other things will be added unto you."
- Jesus Christ in Matthew 6:33

When you and I seek to make direct conscious contact with the kingdom of God's Spirit-Mind-Love-Life Presence within the heart and mind of each of us through prayer and meditation, we are using the greatest God-given gift and power that was ever given to all humanity. As we pray and make direct conscious contact with God, the Universal Subconscious Mind and Love Spirit within us, we discover that God is the very Source of all our ideas, thoughts, desires, dreams, indeed, our very life, and so we experience 'the peace that passes all understanding.' In our former false ego-centered self consciousness we lived in hell. In other words, our false ego-identity consisted of 'me, myself, and I.' We falsely thought we knew it all, and consciously separated ourselves from our Father-Mother God, our neighbor, and all creation.

Now that we have humbly chosen to let go of our false ego-identity consciousness, and turned to God in prayer to deliver us from that hellish state of 'ego-separation', we willingly reconnect to our Father's Universal Master-Mind-Love Consciousness.

We experience the Truth and Freedom that God can, and does, totally transform our lives from within by forgiving us all our mistakes, healing all our diseases, redeeming our lives from destruction and crowning us with loving kindness and tender mercies.   We also wake up to the fact that God has a tailor-made love dream-plan and purpose for each and every one our lives, and that it is nothing less than our heart's desire.   God's will for us as we turn to Him in prayer and meditation turns out to be nothing less than what we would have always loved to be, to do and to have to fulfill our lives and be in tune with God's will for us.

All our ideas, thoughts, desires and dreams, and all the spiritual mental powers we have to fulfill our lives come from God, the Universal Subconscious Master-Mind Love-Spirit within us all.   We can never be separated from God, for in Him, that Infinite Mind and Boundless Love Spirit, "we all live and move and have our being." So now we better understand why a finite mind who tries to live separated from his Creator, his Father-Mother God, Infinite Intelligence and Boundless Love is a fool who lives all alone in the prison of his ego-self powerlessness, loneliness, and fear, guilt and shame-ridden life.   Now we have found a solution.   We turn to a Power greater than ourselves through daily prayer and meditation, and in the Secret Place of our heart and mind kingdom, or subconscious mind, we meet with God and ask to change us from within, and shape and mold us into His God-image and likeness.

Here, in our Secret Place we share our love for one another and ask God to guide us to do His will and individualize His good God thoughts, words, love purpose and deeds for this day and all our lives.   As we are still in His Loving Presence, and wait upon Him trustingly, His still small voice speaks to our inner spirit-mind-heart and reveals His will and love-dream-vision-mission for our lives.   God loves us so very much and willingly answers all our prayers.   God provides us with the inspirational ideas, guidance and strength we need each day to see clearly what we need to do and how to do it.   God works in us to mold, shape and transform our consciousness into His Spirit-Mind-Love-Life Consciousness, so that we gain our new and true identity as His sons and daughters.   "I will put my Spirit-Mind-Love-Life within you and you shall be reborn, renewed, and transformed by the renewing of your mind."

"Before they call, I will answer." "With God all things are possible."

THROUGH PRAYER AND FAITH AND LOVE IN GOD YOU ACHIEVE YOUR DREAMS!

God answers all our prayers when we listen attentively and follow through on His inspirational guidance to grow, to live and to love by sharing our unique gifts and talents with and for the love of all humanity. All God's love, wisdom and power are available to us all the time to overcome or rise above all our difficulties, and live in the glorious freedom of His Loving Presence, Peace and Power as His sons and daughters at one with all. Truly God, Love does such things! Pray and let God's will and love dream purpose for your life be done in you and through you, and as you. As you make your daily conscious contact with your Father-Mother God through prayer and meditation every day, you will quickly learn how to overcome and let go of all your former false ego-consciousness of limiting ideas and beliefs. Indeed by putting on the Universal God Mind-Love Consciousness within you, you will be a new inner-Spirit guided person. You will claim your God-given spiritual mental faculties, laws and powers as a son or daughter. You will be what Jesus learned and demonstrated for us all, 'the light of the world, the salt of the earth.'

LOVE LESSONS TO REMEMBER

There is only One God, the Universal Subconscious Master Mind-Love Spirit Consciousness which individualizes in each and all people, and all creation.

We come to God to change our ego-consciousness, and to be at one with God-Consciousness and claim our powers as sons and daughters of God.

Without prayer and faith and love it is impossible to please our Father-Mother God.

To you that believe in your God-given consciousness, all things are possible.

The universe is owned and operated by a loving God who guides and loves us all.

It is your Father's good pleasure to give you His Kingdom- Consciousness. God gives you Himself to be happy, joyous, prosperous, and free as His son or daughter.

It is God's will that you claim your inheritance and God-given powers to achieve all your dreams and desires for the love and good of all God-Humanity.

God's will for you is really your heart's desire, exactly what you would have always loved to do and to be and to have in your life. We all have unlimited God-potential.

You are praying all the time through your daily thoughts and dream desires.

Praying is asking God for what you need and desire and to claim your God-given consciousness, identity and spiritual mental powers as a son or daughter of God.

Meditation is listening to God's inner spirit guidance, the still small voice within your subconscious mind, giving you the inspiration you need for the solution, the answer to your prayer.

The Law of Supply and Demand is the two ends of the same thing. We must ask knowing that God has already heard us and that our supply is already assured.

Desire in your heart is God calling you to come up higher because He has need of you, and wants to give you all you need, indeed Himself, to fulfill your life.

God seeks and wants to individualize and express Himself through you and as you.

There is only one God, the Universal Master-Mind-Love-Spirit that everyone prays to and receives from.

God's will for us is to be happy, joyous, prosperous and free by being about His business for the love and good of all God-Humanity as His sons and daughters.

MEDITATION

(in U.S. Andersen's book "Three Magic Words"

Here in solitude, in this time of prayer, peace and meditation, I withdraw deep within the silent recesses of my being to a Secret Place of complete calm. Slowly the world retreats from around me, until finally I am alone. Walled away from all noise and strife there is nothing but me. I am not body; I am not thought; I am not experience; I am not the past, present or future. I simply am. Across my conscious mind comes a constant procession of thoughts and I observe them. I do not make up these thoughts. I know they come from God, the Universal Subconscious Mind, and I watch as they are presented to me. I slow the train of my thoughts. I examine each of them, then let go, neither accepting nor rejecting. On and on the thoughts come, and I ask myself "Who is it that observes this?" And I hear the answer, "You are Spirit, always have been, and always will be – you observe," and you understand. Divorced from body, thought, and experience, I still exist as I always must. Here is my true self, a thing independent of all but Spirit, a contemplative "I," which only observes and chooses from the thoughts that cross my consciousness. Whatever I choose to affirm is mine. Whatever I choose to deny, or reject, will never touch me. I only observe and accept, and all things are added unto me by a Power greater than myself, which leaps to acknowledge my faith and my decision. I sense such warmth and security as might overflow the world. I sense a fusion of my being with the great Universal Subconscious Mind-Love-Spirit of God. I sense the Presence of my loving Father-Mother God who knows no wrath, and does all things at our bidding. I am One with God, Divine Spirit, Infinite Mind-Intelligence and Boundless Love, Life, Truth, Law, Beauty and Wisdom. I claim my inheritance as a son or daughter of God and the power to make direct conscious contact with my loving God-Creator.

RECOMMENDED READINGS

Lessons in Truth, by H. Emilie Cady, Published by Unity School of Christianity, 1946.

The Power of Constructive Thinking, by Emmet Fox, Published by Harper Collins, 1932.

The Amazing Laws of Cosmic Mind Power, by Joseph Murphy, Published by Parker Publishing Company Inc., 1965.

Three Magic Words, by U.S. Andersen, Published by Wilshire Book Company, 1954.

CHAPTER TWELVE

STEP CHOICE 12: PASSING ON GOD'S SPIRITUAL LAWS AND POWERS OF MIND TO OTHERS

Having had a spiritual awakening by God setting us free from our false ego-self identity to God-Consciousness as a result of these faith step-choices, we recovered our true spiritual mental identity, faculties and laws of mind as sons and daughters of God. We chose to share this good news in order to free other egotists separated from God, and to practice these laws or principles in all our affairs.

AWAKENING TO THE LOVE LESSONS OF NEW THOUGHT SPIRITUALITY & THE SCIENCE OF MIND OR SPIRIT

Having had a spiritual awakening as a result of taking these spiritual step choices that we have freely chosen to do, we came to have faith in God and attune our finite conscious mind with God's Universal Subconscious Master Mind-Love-Spirit. As we did this, we awoke to our true spiritual mental identity, faculties, and laws of mind, love and life as sons and daughters of God. As we let God's Infinite Intelligence and Boundless Love Presence guide our heart and mind kingdom - our thoughts, ideas, words, and dream desires through the power of prayer and meditation - we found the power to rise above and overcome our old, false, ego-world-self identity with its negative and limiting fear-based beliefs and behaviors, or addictions, and experienced the glorious freedom of our new-found God-Consciousness. We became inner-Spirit guided by God, and no longer ego-centered, or outer-authority directed.

As we chose to pray, trust, and listen more and more to God's Spirit-Mind-Love Presence within us, we came to realize that we are never alone, and that God has given us the spiritual mental powers and laws of creative thought and imagination to form and shape and mold our own lives in tune with His will and purpose, and to individualize and express His ideas and dream desires for each and all of us for the love and good of all humanity. There is only one God, the Universal Subconscious Master-Mind-Love-Spirit who creates for us exactly what our conscious mind thinks and believes and impresses upon It, and this is true of all people worldwide.

As we learn to discipline the thoughts and feelings we allow to enter our heart and mind kingdom, by practicing a daily mental diet of affirming only good God thoughts, and denying entry to false, negative thoughts and beliefs, we wake up to the fact that the law of life is the law of belief, and that as we think in our heart, or subconscious mind, God, the Universal Subconscious Mind Spirit within all, creates in our outer physical world conditions. In fact, God awakens us to the truth that our inner world of ideas, thoughts, feelings, desires and faith beliefs control and shape our outer life experiences and conditions. We become aware that we become what we think about all day long; that we are our beliefs expressed. We realize that we live in a mental universe that is controlled by spiritual mental laws, and that the spiritual mental law of life for all people is 'as within, so without.'

When we choose to admit the greatest lie, or addiction of the ages, that our false ego-self finite mind is not God, and self-sufficient unto itself; and we surrender our false ego-self to God's Infinite Intelligence and Boundless Love; and consecrate our will and our lives to God's will and purpose for our life; we find our heart's desire. We wake up to the Truth that sets us free – that we are each created and sent into this world to individualize and express God's ideas or dream desires in us and as us. It is in this inner-dependent relationship between our conscious mind with God's Universal Subconscious Master Mind that we have our greatest freedom of thinking and acting. Here, we now know where all our ideas, thoughts and dream desires come from, and how God's Creative Master Mind-Spirit energy manifests into form from our thoughts and faith convictions into our physical reality right here on earth for the good of all. We realize that our Father-Mother God is the Source and Substance of all our good, and continuously inspires, enlightens, and empowers us to achieve whatever God calls us to be, to do and to have for the good of all humanity. As we surrender our finite ego-self, that Emerson called 'our bloated nothingness,' to God and let Him guide, will, love and work through us we are renewed in spirit, mind and body.

As we choose to let God's words, ideas and desires incarnate in us day by day, by daily prayer and meditation, we come to realize that as sons and daughters of God we can achieve whatever our heart's desires can conceive of, for they are God-given desires. We become the free, creative spiritual beings God created us to be, and we go forth in faith to achieve our God-given dreams and destiny for the love of all. Having been renewed in spirit, mind and body by our Father-Mother God's Loving Presence, Peace and Power, we are compelled to pass on this good news to all our brothers and sisters worldwide. We are so filled with God's Spirit-Mind-Love-Life that we must share the miracles that God has worked in our lives, and that this is possible for all persons who surrender their small ego-centered life, and in faith consecrate their lives and will to God's will and purpose.

In this book we have introduced you to the 12 steps of the Circle of Prayer to help you manifest your God-given dreams, as well as, to the 12 step creative attitudes of mind you need to help you maintain your new spiritual mental identity as sons and daughters of God, and focus on in fulfilling your God-given dreams for an abundant life. This book is our way of sharing with you the amazing miracles God has worked in our lives and the lives of millions of other recovering egotists. The love lessons taught here will benefit all people worldwide, no matter what their creed, color, sex or cultural beliefs may be, for they are concerned with teaching universal God-given spiritual mental faculties and laws of mind, love and life that are common to all people worldwide. This spiritual program reveals our universal God-given spiritual mental powers and laws of mind, and the twelve step choices that we each must take to achieve our new God-Conscious identity as sons and daughters of God.

The New Thought Spirituality and Science of Mind laws or principles we share here have been passed on to us through many recovered egotists, and mystic sages like Jesus Christ through the ages, and by the grace of God it is our great joy and calling to share this good news with you who hunger and thirst to know, love and serve God with all your heart, mind, soul and strength, and love your neighbor as yourself.

This burst of New Thought Spiritual energy is uniting people all over the world today because it unites us all under One God, One Divine Subconscious Master-Mind-Spirit who dwells in us all as equal-souled sons and daughters of God, who are all subject to the same spiritual mental faculties and laws of mind, love and life. Religion has the unfortunate tendency to separate people not only from God, but also from our neighbors and indeed all creation by their own man-made, and false ego-centered and outer authority-directed theologies, which have kept God's people in bondage for centuries. It is not what Jesus Christ and other sages taught us at all.

Today we are waking up to this Truth that we are individualized expressions of God, spiritual beings manifesting God's ideas and purposes through our God-given power of prayer, creative thought and expression. The desires of our True Spiritual-Self are united as one in our heart, mind and soul. With this renewal of our true spiritual self-identity, we share God's dream desire and purpose for ourselves and all people, so we can live in free, happy, joyous, and loving relationships, careers, and environment. We begin to see the power of God's work radiating through each and all of us, as we realize that we are sons and daughters of an infinite powerful Father-Mother God who is love, wisdom and intelligence and has no boundaries. We realize that we are spiritual beings and that the Spirit-Mind-Love-Life of the Lord lives in us all as sons and daughters of one Father-Mother God.

In practicing and living in our new state of God-Mind-Love-Consciousness we will no longer suffer the false ego-consciousness of separation, loneliness, fear, limitation and anxiety. We now know a new freedom and a new happiness. In being God-centered and God-guided we are living and implementing the greatest law of the mind, Love, and let us now go forward, upward, and God-ward as we go forth to achieve our God-given dreams and desires. As we practice loving God and our neighbor as ourselves, we are practicing God Consciousness in us all, and letting our spiritual freedom path radiate out from us as sons and daughters of God.

LOVE LESSONS TO REMEMBER

There is only one God, the Universal Divine Subconscious Master-Mind-Love-Spirit in which all people live, and move, and have our being.

You are a son or daughter of God and the Spirit-Mind-Love-Life of God is individualized in you and as you.

Our thoughts, ideas, dreams and desires are God-given, and are Energy or Spirit.

With God in us all, all things are possible to us.

We are spiritual beings in human form, here to fulfill God's loving will for our lives.

Ego-self is our false-self guided by our outer senses and by outer-world-authorities.

Our Spiritual-Self is our True God-Self identity when our conscious mind is at-one with God, the Universal Subconscious Master-Mind-Love-Spirit within us all.

In meditation we learn to listen to God's inner voice within our subconscious mind.

In prayer we make direct conscious contact with God. We ask God to provide us with all we need to fulfill His will and purpose for our lives for the love of all.

All prayers and desires are always answered according to our faith in God.

MEDITATION

We reveal our true Spiritual-Self identity as a son or daughter of our Father-Mother God's Spirit-Mind-Love-Life within us by working the step choices outlined in our spiritual growth program. By trusting and allowing God to transform us by the renewing of our mind, we are no longer conformed to our false outer-authority directed ego-self. As we surrender to a Power greater than ourselves He begins to change us from within. Our ideas, thoughts, beliefs are transformed and renewed, and as a result our outer world experiences are changed accordingly. Having experienced a spiritual awakening as a result of taking these spiritual mental step choices, and incorporating the spiritual mental laws they teach into our heart and mind kingdom, we feel compelled to pass on this miracle-working knowledge; and the healing our Creator has done for us to other ego-centered egotists. To all people who are willing and desire to be changed, and want to discover their true spiritual identity and powers as sons and daughters of God. As we share our love and faith with others, we bear witness to the Truth of what our Creator God has done for us, and we lovingly choose to pass on this good news to all. It is through our inner-dependence on God that we are truly independent of the good opinion of others, and that we have the freedom of choice to live life in peace, harmony and love with all God's creatures. The more we share the more we learn about ourselves, for in giving we receive the blessings and bounty of God's abundant love life. Love does such things!

RECOMMENDED READINGS

Three Magic Words, by U.S. Andersen, Published by Wilshire Publishing Company, 1954.

The Amazing Laws of Cosmic Mind Power, by Joseph Murphy, Published byParker Publishing Company, Inc., 1965